FANGS OF DEATH

Advance praise for the book

'A remarkable example of writing intricately about police procedure without compromising on thrill. The father-son duo has added another deft piece of crime writing to their impressive array.'

– **S. Hussain Zaidi**, author of *Black Friday*

'The fabulous true crime writer duo of Aloke and Maanas Lal brings one of the most intriguing cases to book. It reads like a classic Poirot or Holmes whodunnit—except this is a true story. Fact is stranger than fiction.'

– **Anirban Bhattacharyya**, author of *The Deadly Dozen*, Creator-Producer of *Savdhaan India*

'As the DGP of the state, I had the occasion to supervise the investigation...I know this book will be an instant hit for common people and for law enforcement officers.'

– **Lokanath Behera**, Former DGP, Kerala

FANGS OF DEATH

The True Story of the Kerala Snake Bite Murder

Maanas Lal
Aloke Lal

AMARYLLIS

AMARYLLIS

An imprint of Manjul Publishing House Pvt. Ltd.
• C-16, Sector 3, Noida, Uttar Pradesh 201301, India
Website: www.manjulindia.com
Registered Office:
• 10, Nishat Colony, Bhopal 462 003 – India
Distribution Centres
Ahmedabad, Bengaluru, Bhopal, Chennai, Hyderabad, Kolkata, Mumbai, Noida, Pune

Fangs of Death by Maanas Lal and Aloke Lal

This paperback edition first published in India in 2024

ISBN 978-93-5543-369-5

Cover design: Bhavi Mehta

Printed and bound in India by Thomson Press (India) Ltd.

The book is based on the judgment of the sessions court, police station records and conversations with investigators. Some elements in the story have been dramatised for the reader's pleasure. This narrative is not intended to in any way influence the ongoing legal process in the higher judiciary.

To,
the silent but telling contributions of forensic experts
in solving crime

The book is based on the judgment of the sessions court, police station records and conversations with investigators. Some elements in the story have been dramatised for the reader's pleasure. This narrative is not intended to in any way influence the ongoing legal process in the higher judiciary.

CONTENTS

PROLOGUE

The television serial *Snake Wranglers* aired on National Geographic in the year 2000. One of the authors of this book, Maanas Lal, was all of ten at the time. The only thing he found more fascinating than the serpents slithering across the screen in the thirteen half-hour episodes were the wranglers who handled them. He went on to prepare a scrapbook full of information about snakes, their habitats, and their favourite prey. This love for the reptile continued to grow as the years rolled on and a small herpetology section became a part of our in-house library. This is where the germ of writing this book was truly born—several years before the crime took place, and not out of fear, but from an unadulterated love for snakes.

A name which stood out among those who appeared on the show was that of herpetologist Gerry Martin. He was National Geographic's first Indian adventurer. The episode in which he featured was ironically titled 'Fangs to Fortune'. In the episode, he travels to the remote village of Patia in Bhubaneswar, Odisha, in an effort to convince the local snake charmers to give up the practice of de-fanging snakes. He goes on to teach them the art of milking snake venom and marketing it for the production of anti-venom.

Maanas was so impacted by the sensitivity with which Gerry handled the fabled creatures that he began to draw snakes instead of swans in his art class! Several years later, while working at Infosys, Maanas came across The Gerry Martin Project (TGMP) based in Hunsur, Karnataka. The idea behind TGMP was to bring all of Gerry's conservation and education work under one umbrella by putting together a team of like-minded people. The focus of the project in those days was on studying the Russell's viper using radio telemetry to 'shed light on the human-snake dynamics and the ecology of the snake in a human-dominated landscape.'[1] Maanas considered joining the project as a volunteer several times, but the mundane contours of corporate life kept him busy.

When an article about the Uthra murder case reached us through a WhatsApp group of which we are both members, it immediately caught Maanas' eye. It was an opportunity to not just write about the tribulations of a woman who was differently abled, but also one to shed light on the innocence of the snakes involved in the crime. In the penning of this book, a lot of care has been taken to depict snakes as equal victims of human greed and depravity. It is a doff of the hat to conservationists like Gerry Martin.

---

1 Purva Variyar, 'The Snake and I: Decoding the Work of Gerry Martin,' 15 June 2022, https://roundglasssustain.com/heroes/gerry-martin-snakes-wildlife-india

TURNING THE ALLY

Behind (almost) every despicable criminal is an ally.

The preceding sentence is truer than many would like to believe. The translation of criminal intent into criminal action often needs a catalyst, and for the catalyst to be a co-conspirator is quite common. Much like Sherlock Holmes had the allyship of James Watson, Douglas Clark would never have become one half of the Sunset Strip Killers[2] without a Carol Bundy. The human propensity to look the other way for reasons of financial gratification or abject depravity is a sobering thought.

While anyone who willingly partakes in a criminal act deserves to be punished, investigators sometimes resort to the ploy of turning one or more of the conspirators into approvers.[3]

---

2 In the summer of 1980, murderous atrocities in West Hollywood, California, committed by an odd couple led to their notoriety as the Sunset Strip Killers.

3 The term 'approver' is neither defined nor used in the Criminal Procedure Code (CPC), but is usually applied to a person, supposed to be either directly or indirectly concerned with or privy to an offence, to whom a pardon is granted under Section 337 of the CPC (Section 306 of the new code) with a view to securing his/her testimony against other persons guilty of the offence. The

Perhaps even law, for all its inherent logic, leaves these criminals to the promise of a punishment in the afterlife.

July 2020

Chavarukavu Suresh was a mini sensation in Kerala. His snake wrangling videos had gone viral on YouTube and his channel S.K. Media 2255 was the talk of several towns in God's own country, particularly those where venomous snakes were commonly spotted. That Kerala has a rich snake population added to the scalability of the channel and its subscriber base. But the recent surge in Suresh's viewership was for unenviable reasons. He was in the headlines for being hauled up as a co-conspirator in a sensational murder case.

Suresh's profession was fraught with risks. His fame had come at a high price—the middle finger in his right hand was deformed. It was distinctive damage caused by the bite of a Russell's viper. One thing was for certain though: Suresh was no cold-blooded criminal. And yet, he had managed to land up on the wrong side of an interrogation table in a claggy room for the umpteenth time in three months. For nearly an hour, he had been staring at the mossy walls of the interrogation room whose varying hues and abstract patterns had a hypnotic effect. His mind was playing games with him even before an interrogator had walked in.

---

procedure laid down in Section 337 (Section 306 of the new code) has often been resorted to in this state in cases of organised crime like dacoities, when no independent evidence is available to bring the offenders to book.

In one corner of the room was a baton. It was the only polished object in the room, and the sheen of the Kerala Police emblem on it stood out against the dingy backdrop. It was a foreboding sight for Suresh. He was nervously feeling his knees and ankles. The anticipated pain of the baton striking his body had found its way to his jet-black irises even before someone actually picked it up.

A. Ashokan, the deputy superintendent of police (DySP) of the District Crime Branch, Kollam rural district, strode into the interrogation room with the nonchalance of a veteran. He was well acquainted with the subject and was aware that he might not need much persuading to divulge the truth. It had taken just a fleeting glance for his experienced eyes to sum up Suresh's prevailing state of mind.

'Why did you do it?' Ashokan asked Suresh as he pulled out the chair on the opposite side of the table.

'Sir?' Suresh's frightened voice was all but drowned in the squeak of the chair as Ashokan sat himself down.

The standard expression on Ashokan's face could be best described as being matter-of-fact. This was a great aid to his work as an interrogator, a God's gift of sorts. Suresh had already started according all sorts of meaning, most of them negative, to the blankness on the cop's familiar face.

'Hmmm…why did you do it?' Ashokan demanded.

Suresh managed a quizzical look in response.

'Look Suresh, you can trust me,' Ashokan said in a comforting tone, 'and frankly, you have little choice!' The second part of the sentence was assertive.

'Sir, I am so sorry. I did not know things would come to this,' Suresh mumbled.

Ashokan responded with a long stare before flicking an eyebrow as a signal for Suresh to continue talking.

'I hardly know him, sir. I did not know he was going to do this. I swear!'

'I am close to retirement, Suresh. I have worn this khaki for much longer than the lack of grey in my hair suggests. I have lost count of the number of interrogations I have conducted. You know me well by now. Do you think you can take me for a ride? In which snake-pit were you hiding if you are so innocent?' Ashokan's pitch rose through the roof. 'Uthra has been mercilessly murdered by a weapon that *you* supplied! We already have your statement on record. We have also collected a lot of evidence in the last three months. Do you understand what that means in a court of law?' Ashokan demanded and then briefly glanced at the baton in the room.

The change in Ashokan's demeanour rattled Suresh. He could see that the seasoned cop meant business. His eyes were now fixed on the baton, and fear was writ large and clear on his shrunken face. He felt as if he had aged greatly in the hour gone by. Even the dreaded reptiles he caught for a living had never made him feel this degree of insecurity.

Ashokan had noticed the change in Suresh's expressions and he now introduced an element of equality in the conversation: water. He slipped the small bottle of water that he had been carrying to Suresh's side of the table. Suresh's eyes followed the movement of the bottle intently. When Ashokan indicated that the bottle was for him, Suresh picked it up, drank a sip, and cleared an evidently clogged throat.

Ashokan looked straight into Suresh's eyes. 'Water takes the shape of its container,' he said. 'A conspirator in a heinous crime also carries the same dark outline as the perpetrator. But you still have a chance to save yourself and your family, Suresh. Do not allow Sooraj's shadow to darken your and your daughter's future.'

Ashokan then got up and walked over to Suresh. He kept a comforting hand on his shoulder and said, 'Your prison mates have told me that you keep crying all day. Nearly two months have gone by since your and Sooraj's incarceration. Your body languages are a study in contrast. He keeps to himself and indirectly boasts of his exploits. You, on the other hand, talk about being trapped and helpless. You have also given us useful information about the murder weapon, or should I say weapons? We have no gaps or loopholes in our case, but the SIT[4] feels you deserve some mercy.' Ashokan leaned in, 'Speak the truth, Suresh. Take the only lifeline you have.'

'Sir, I don't know where to start and I do not want to implicate myself. I have been evasive so far because Sooraj threatened me. He said that I will also be charged with murder. It is only after much thought that I have decided to come clean. My daughter feels that the cops will help me if I am honest,' Suresh responded. He looked like he was on the verge of tears.

'I am here to walk you through the process. Do not worry about self-implication. Let us look at what we both know

---

4 Special Investigation Team.

indisputably. Sooraj approached you for the first time on 12 February. Our cyber expert has confirmed that he called you from a phone which is now included in the evidence we have. What was the purpose of that first call?' Ashokan asked. He understood that Suresh needed some nudging in a definitive direction.

'Sir, he said he was a fan. He wanted me to forward videos of my most daring snake rescues to him. He claimed that he had a deep-seated respect for snake wranglers. He also told me that he was an official with HDFC Bank.'

'Hmmm…he lowered your defences right at the outset,' Ashokan surmised.

'I don't know how to express this, sir. It felt good to be acknowledged for what is otherwise a largely thankless job. A small crowd gathers every time we rescue venomous snakes, but the sense of awe that people have for the creatures completely overshadows the heroism of the rescuer. Once the snake is confined, the crowd dissipates much quicker than it gathered, often without even a fleeting word of gratitude.' Suresh looked out of the sole window in the room. 'It felt nice to be hailed a hero. For once, it felt like I was doing something worthwhile.'

'I can understand. Even the police often take help from your ilk but they seldom share the credit for a successful rescue. The names of the rescuers are rarely, if ever, mentioned in press releases. Not even a sliver of the acknowledgement is shared. The risk-to-reward ratio just does not add up. You never know when a slight let up in reflexes might lead to a loss of limb or even life.' Ashokan's words were laden with genuine empathy for he knew the demands of a high-risk job all too well. 'What happened next?'

'I forwarded some videos to Sooraj after our first telephonic conversation. He made it a point to keep in touch after that. He was fascinated by snakes and we chatted about them frequently. He wanted to know everything—how their scales feel, what they eat, where their venom secreting glands are, and so on. He was particularly interested in learning the art of capturing and relocating snakes. It sounded like he had a genuine love for the creature.'

'Suresh, I think that you are a person with depth. Tell me then, how did you get caught up in Sooraj's web of crime?' Ashokan asked in an even tone.

'Sir, after our first few conversations, Sooraj invited me to conduct an awareness workshop. He said that knowledge about the local snake population would be of great value to the people in his locality. I saw merit in his request.' Suresh was struggling through his sentences. 'I was so foolish. I believed him. A little flattery got him everywhere!'

'Yes, we have information about the workshop on record. Suresh, I know that going through everything again is hard for you. But this is also your only chance at redemption.' Ashokan was slowly wading his way into Suresh's circle of trust. 'What happened at the workshop?'

'Initially, I told Sooraj that I had no snakes available for a demonstration. He said he was willing to wait. A few days later, I rescued a four-foot-long Russell's viper from the vicinity of a building owned by the Oozhayikkodu Ayyappa Temple Trust. The rescue was live-streamed on Facebook and Sooraj saw it too.

He called me up a little later and persuaded me to use this snake for hosting the workshop. His enterprise impressed me and I decided to hold the workshop. In the meantime, I informed Raju, the rescue van driver, and Premjith, my partner, about the awareness class. I spoke to Sooraj a little later and told him jokingly that I would charge Rs10,000 for the work. To my surprise, Sooraj was okay with the price. He promised to arrange the money and requested me to hold the workshop early in the morning. He thought a greater crowd would gather in the wee hours. After a little back and forth, we finalised the date and the time—26 February at 5.30 a.m.'

Ashokan stood up suddenly at this point in time. 'You are doing well, Suresh. But I would like to have a word with my superiors before we resume our conversation. I will be back shortly.'

After two gruelling months of incarceration and multiple rounds of interrogation, Suresh was finally talking. Ashokan knew that the prosecution's case was going to hinge heavily on Suresh's testimony in court. He felt that an added incentive would make Suresh's testimony and his will to divulge information about the case even sharper. The reason for the break in the interrogation was precisely this. Ashokan recalled that Mohan Raj, the public prosecutor, had suggested that Suresh would best serve the purpose of the case as an approver. He decided to talk to his superiors in the police force about exploring this possibility.

Ashokan placed a call to S. Hari Sankar, the superintendent of police (SP). It took him a couple of attempts to get through.

'Sir, I have an update on Uthra's case,' Ashokan got straight to the point.

'Go on,' the SP responded.

'Sir, the co-accused, Suresh, is willing to spill the beans. He is, however, concerned about his family, especially his young daughter. Can we cut a deal with him?' Ashokan inquired.

'What exactly are you suggesting?'

'Sir, Mohan Raj feels that if we make Suresh an approver in the case, we have a very high likelihood of achieving a conviction against the prime accused. Our case is almost entirely based on circumstantial evidence right now. But if Suresh becomes our key witness, the defence lawyer will have very little wriggle room.' Ashokan's voice had a strong hint of surety.

There was silence for a minute or so before the SP spoke again.

'Let me get back to you on this.' Hari Sankar cut the call and immediately dialled the number of Director General of Police (DGP) Lokanath Behera.

Behera belonged to the 1985 batch of the Indian Police Service (IPS). His in-depth understanding of criminal procedure was acknowledged by all his colleagues. A founding member of the National Investigation Agency (NIA), he was also instrumental in modernising the Kerala police force and equipping it with modern vehicles and state-of-the-art small arms and non-lethal weaponry.

'Tell me, Hari Sankar,' Behera asked pointedly.

'Sir, Ashokan called with an update on the Uthra murder case. Suresh has agreed to confess.'

'The snake wrangler?'

'Yes, sir. Ashokan thinks making him an approver in the case will greatly help our cause. He is not a hardened criminal and he also seems to be an unwilling accomplice. So far, he has been forthcoming with information which led to the unearthing of some critical evidence.'

Known to make quick decisions, Behera responded, 'I see where Ashokan is coming from. Let us try to get an approval from the chief judicial magistrate. The process prescribed in law is a little complicated.'

'Sir, I have a request. I would like to get Anoop Krishna for recording the confession.'

'Isn't he posted as the station house officer (SHO) of some police station in Thiruvananthapuram?' Behera inquired.

'Yes, sir. But he is the best man for the job.'

'I trust your well-honed instincts. Get it done!' the DGP said.

'Thank you, sir. Jai Hind!' Hari Sankar sounded triumphant.

Soon after this, Hari Sankar called Ashokan and told him to keep Suresh in the right headspace as they readied everything for recording his confession. He also called Anoop Krishna and asked him to assist the team in getting the confession.

Ashokan returned to the interrogation room with a cup of coffee in his hands. He had an intricate understanding of coffee beans and prided himself on the degree to which he knew the art of brewing. He always got the temperature right. Neither the lukewarm servings of multinational coffee chains nor the piping hot creations that came out of home kitchens were to his liking.

As he sipped on the delectable drink, he managed a reassuring smile for Suresh.

Unable to control his curiosity after noticing Ashokan's favourable body language, Suresh asked, 'What happened, sir? Is there some good news? What did your superiors say?'

Ashokan took an unusually loud sip of the coffee before breaking his studied silence, 'Suresh, I have an offer that you can't refuse!'

Unaware of the original Al Pacino reference from *The Godfather* and perhaps in no position to reference pop culture, Suresh asked, 'Sir, I do not understand. What has happened?'

'Suresh, you will not miss seeing your daughter grow. You will get a second chance at life. I have just spoken to the SP. The good officer has agreed to make you an approver in the case!' Ashokan's face had a look of immense pride as he made this announcement.

'Sir, I do not know what that means. Please excuse my ignorance,' Suresh said nervously.

'It's simple. You will have to narrate the entire story in court as our key witness. We will prep you for the trial and make sure that all your facts are in place. SHO Anoop Krishna, one of our department's sharpest minds, is on his way to record your confession. In other words, as long as you tell him the whole story and agree to turn on Sooraj, we can get you off the hook. Wouldn't that be nice?'

Suresh stared at Ashokan in disbelief. Then he looked out of the window again. He felt his knees tremble, and then the sound of his stomach rumbling made its way to Ashokan's ears too. Suresh's face turned red and he let out a small sigh. Ashokan could see that in the space of a minute, his suspect had gone through an entire gamut of emotions.

'Sir, is this actually possible? You think I can walk free?' Suresh asked incredulously.

'Yes, you can. You will have to live up to the promise you have shown me in today's questioning session. You have a logical stream of thought and I can make out that you were in the wrong place at the wrong time. Go through the events leading up to Uthra's death with a fine-toothed comb. Tell Anoop Krishna her story, right down to the last detail. Include everything you have told me after your arrest and all that you haven't. Remember that plea deals are subject to market risks. Read the paperwork carefully before investing your faith in them.' Ashokan peppered the hope he was handing out to Suresh with words of caution.

'I will tell him everything, sir. As long as I get to parent my daughter, I am willing to turn on Sooraj. My mind is without fear now that the dream of going back to my family is a real possibility. Thank you, sir.'

Anoop Krishna arrived the next day without any fanfare. He told the duty officer that he wanted to see Ashokan. The two of them were soon sitting across from each other.

'The SP has a lot of faith in you.' Ashokan smiled at Krishna.

'Sir, I have had the honour of serving under him. He is a kind person,' Krishna responded.

'I am sure you have been briefed about the case?'

'Yes, sir. I am familiar with the facts and have read through the case files in detail. I have clearly understood the chain of events. Is there anything you would like to add?'

'Not really. I am sure you will be instrumental in helping us get a conviction, Krishna. One thing I would advise you to do is to take Suresh's daughter into confidence. She is his greatest weakness and also his biggest strength,' Ashokan said evenly.

'I will keep that in mind, sir. Thank you!'

'All the best!'

Instead of heading to Suresh's cell, however, Krishna now decided to visit his daughter Sona Suresh first. He went to her college and learnt from her teachers that she had been facing a hard time ever since Suresh had been arrested. He also asked her classmates about her general demeanour and learnt that she was a straight arrow.

Krishna then visited Suresh's house in Kalluvathukkal. He spoke to his daughter there and asked her to continue being a source of strength for her father. He told her that it was only through her efforts that Suresh could soon be a free man. Sona promised to help in the investigation and visited Suresh immediately after.

Sona's persuasion had the desired effect. Suresh moved an application to the Sub Divisional Magistrate Court, Punalur stating that he wanted to give a full disclosure statement. Based on this, Ashokan moved an application under Section 306 of the Criminal Procedure Code before the chief judicial magistrate (CJM), Kollam to make Suresh an approver in the case. Pursuant to the application, the CJM issued a production warrant for Suresh.

Suresh was produced in court for the first time on 13 July 2020. The CJM warned Suresh of the risks involved in making a statement and asked him questions as mandated in the Criminal Rules of Practice. She remanded him in custody and gave him time to reflect till 16 July. On 16 July, she examined him in the court hall after the door was shut. Suresh was determined to confess and earn his way out of the quicksand he was in.

For several hours which stretched across several days, Suresh's statement under Section 164[5] of the Criminal Procedure Code was recorded. This statement was going to be the key to unlocking the secrets of a ruthless criminal mind.

Interrogators come in all shapes and sizes. While some do use size to their advantage, most skilled are those who rely on their grey matter. The ability to take dabs from the dark greys where criminal minds often dwell is a hard skill to master. Some repeat tried and tested sequences like establishing a baseline, building confidence, and compromising mental defences. Others have a knack to go with the flow of the criminal instinct and create abstract scenarios that challenge even the wiliest minds. Such cops would have perhaps made very successful criminals too. It

[5] Section 164(1) of the Criminal Procedure Code, 1973 states that, 'Any metropolitan magistrate or judicial magistrate may, whether or not he has jurisdiction in the case, record any confession or statement made to him in the course of an investigation under this chapter or under any other law for the time being in force, or at any time afterwards before the commencement of the inquiry....'

is the good fortune of the justice system that people like Ashokan and Krishna are found more frequently on its right side.

After Suresh's confession, the SIT started to piece together the entire puzzle surrounding Uthra's murder. The evidence collected in the preceding months pointed to the origins of the final act being rooted in the twin baggage of societal norms and resultant othering. The crime effectively began even before Uthra was married to Sooraj. It was a crime that laid bare the hypocrisy of society and highlighted the risks of remaining mired in tradition.

HAPPILY MARRIED

India is obsessed with the idea of job security. This is not much of a surprise considering the country is still emerging from the financial shambles which the British imperialists had left it in. Although the idea of gainful private employment has caught on substantially since independence, the lure of a monthly government pay cheque still reigns supreme. Most government servants, even those who lack notable merit, manage to scrape through service and in the process, they provide reasonably well for their families. This security makes even doctorate holders settle for gross underemployment as long as life climbs onto a tried and tested track.

The three decades plus of service that most government employees invest makes them attuned to the idea of stability. The first of every month begins with a welcome notification bell that credits not just a salary, but also the sustenance of close to a billion people. The days of the monthly *lifafa* (envelope) may be over, but even now, for a large section of modern and digital India, the thought process is still centred around the idea of cash-in-hand.

Against this backdrop, retirement becomes a forbidden word. The thought of all the security, privileges, and stability vanishing in an instant makes the whole family anxious. From an entry level employee, known very discriminatorily as a Class IV employee within government hierarchy, to the chief secretary, who is the top boss in the Indian Administrative Service (IAS), everyone plans for the inevitable, and in spite of all the planning, also manages to look thoroughly underprepared when the day finally arrives.

It can be said that the seeds of Uthra's murder were sowed at the time of her father's retirement. It was the inflection point where Uthra went from being a child to being a daughter who had to be married off, and the need to find her a husband took centre stage.

January 2018

Vijayasenan had arrived at a crucial juncture in his life. As he craned his neck to read the number of zeros in his retirement cheque, he thought of the many responsibilities he was yet to fulfil. The primary responsibility among these was that of finding a suitable match for his daughter Uthra. While the patriarchal nature of Indian society forces parents into a claustrophobic corner when it comes to looking for a potential groom, Uthra's case was even more challenging. She was differently abled and her intelligence quotient (IQ) was well below average. All the myths and the differential treatment that accompany any form of disability in the background of patriarchy make what society considers a normal progression of life virtually impossible for those like Uthra. Kerala has traditionally been seen as a matrilineal state with an even gender ratio and a superior literacy rate, but the rust of generations of imbalance takes an infinite amount of time to wear off.

Manimekhala, Uthra's mother, shared her husband's concerns. She had superannuated as the head mistress of a government upper primary school and she was now keen on finding a groom whose family would support Uthra once Vijayasenan and she were no longer around. Adding to her worries were her own chronic health issues.

The term *dalal* (broker) is usually associated with material wealth. Brokers have to work ruthlessly within the small profit margins that the deals involving property, stocks, artefacts, and the likes offer. In India, a lot of these transactions are done off the record and the payments are almost exclusively limited to cash transactions. To use the term 'broker' for those who help families find suitable matrimonial matches for their children is in itself a sad reality. Built into this is the implicit understanding that a transaction is taking place. Knowing that finding a suitable groom for Uthra would be a tall order, Vijayasenan decided to use the services of a marriage broker. The word that best describes such marriage alliances is compromise. And compromises rarely come without a heavy price!

The broker employed by Vijayasenan was quick on his feet. He found a suitable groom in Sooraj whose family soon visited Uthra's home in Anchal. They approved of the match and things moved at the rate of knots thereon. The engagement was formalised in the early part of 2018 and Uthra's family couldn't have been happier. But shortly after the engagement, Sooraj began to change colours. He started emphasising on Uthra's disability and the challenges that a marriage with her would pose. Sure enough, the solution proposed by him fell squarely within the malfeasant boundaries of dowry.

Uthra's parents were faced with a difficult choice. On the one hand, their differently abled daughter had a real shot at leading as close to normal a life as she possibly could if they acceded to an unlawful but commonplace demand. On the other hand was the prospect of breaking Uthra's heart and risking leaving her alone in a world that already treated her as an outcast!

They decided to visit Sooraj at his home in Parakkodu. On the way, they sought divine blessings at the Sri Mulloor Kulangara Devi Temple. They had faith that God would help them out of the tricky situation they found themselves in. Sooraj's family, however, was upfront about their demands, and there were many of them. They were not really open to any negotiations and were clearly apathetic to any trouble these demands would cause to Uthra's family. Multiple requests by Vijayasenan to reduce the quantum of the dowry were turned down. What little relief Uthra's parents managed to wrangle could barely be called a concession.

The final verbal agreement stood thus: ninety sovereigns[6] of gold ornaments as opposed to the initial demand of hundred, a

[6] One sovereign is equal to 8 gm of gold.

Baleno car in place of the beastly Innova, and Rs 5 lakh in cash as opposed to six.

Sooraj and Uthra's marriage was solemnised on 25 March 2018. The fulfillment of dowry demands invariably leads to greater greed and more demands from the groom and his family. Sooraj's case was no different. His marriage with Uthra was followed by a couple of uneventful months, after which a slew of demands was made.

Under the garb of decorating Uthra's new marital home, several home appliances were first on the list. This demand was then extended to the need for new furniture and the construction of a car shed. Slowly, the specificity of the reasons vanished and the demand was for cash, for the sake of the proper maintenance of Uthra and her new home. This should have served as a warning signal for Uthra's parents. However, their daughter's supposed welfare, prevalent societal norms, and a tacit acceptance of the institution of dowry made them comply with these demands.

Soon, Sooraj's family became a prominent part of the demands. His sister decided to do an MBA degree. Uthra's parents footed the bill for her admission to a local college. The expenses of a tour which she undertook as part of the programme were also borne by Vijayasenan. Sooraj also received Rs 8,000 every month via a wire transfer from Vijayasenan.

There is a tendency in our culture to think of a child as a solution for a marriage which is on the rocks. Seasoned elders often come up with this nugget of advice: *Bachcha kar lo...phir sab theek ho jayega* (have a kid...that will fix everything)!

The numerous logical loopholes in this piece of advice and the lack of scientific evidence do not seem to deter the advice seekers either. Uthra delivered her first baby in the April of 2019. Once again, the hospital bills were Vijayasenan's headache. Uthra's parents hoped that the birth of the child would bring Sooraj and Uthra closer. They even gifted the couple a goat to provide fresh milk to the newborn, and then also got an animal shed constructed for the goat at Sooraj's place.

As it happens in many situations, the age-old wisdom of bridging a broken marriage on the fragile back of a newborn child was trumped by the intentions of a differently determined husband, and now father. Sooraj continued to make Uthra's life miserable. His financial demands kept mounting and so did the toxicity in their relationship.

Things reached a breaking point soon and in January 2020, Uthra requested for the intervention of her family. Her cousin Syamdev and her mother Manimekhala visited her and Sooraj in the hope of resolving their differences. They were shocked at the degree of atrocity that Uthra was dealing with on a daily basis. She faced a barrage of insults from all members of Sooraj's family almost every day. Snide remarks were made about her physical appearance and she was constantly referred to as retarded. She also had to cope with repeated references being made to her not having brought enough dowry and was sometimes even abused physically. Seeing the plight of his sister, Syamdev told Sooraj that a separation would be in order. Sooraj was a mute spectator to this suggestion. This drastically changed when Syamdev started talking about the financial ramifications of a divorce. The thought of having to return all the cash and gold that he had already received from his in-laws made Sooraj apologetic. He promised Syamdev and Manimekhala that no further harm would come to Uthra. Perhaps still burdened by the thought of potential societal shunning in the wake of a divorce, Syamdev and Manimekhala decided to give Sooraj another chance.

Manimekhala was a cancer patient and also had a kidney problem. Apart from Sooraj's insatiable greed, her own medical treatments were proving to be a major financial burden on the family. While she had her daughter's best interest at heart and knew of the extreme abuse she was putting up with, the decision making, when it came to Uthra's immediate welfare, had many rather unfortunate layers to it.

Sooraj never introduced Uthra to even his thickest of friends. He often referred to her as being mentally retarded in a cavalier manner at social gatherings. His aversion towards her was evident. Even Sujith, a childhood friend of Sooraj, was never invited to Sree Surya, Sooraj's house, after the marriage. In fact, he had not even been invited to the wedding. This social seclusion and shunning had made Uthra develop a deep-rooted inferiority complex. Whatever chance she had to brush shoulders with mainstream society had been completely lost in her matrimony. But she continued to live at Sooraj's place. While the family made it difficult for her to even cook for her baby, she was left with little choice. Her life was mired in stalemate. She was destined to live in misery for others were to financially benefit from it. The very nature of society is criminal when it comes to weighing down an already defeated person. Few knew this construct better than Uthra.

HONING IN

There comes a point for every greedy person when the source of their satiation dries up. Their parasitic intentions, however, continue to want more. This is often the case when crimes related to dowry are committed. If a transactional understanding becomes the foundation of a lifelong relationship, any default on a demand for payment is a step towards severing togetherness.

In Sooraj and Uthra's case, love was never in play. In fact, there was a clear aversion that Sooraj harboured towards his wife. He treated her as a necessary nuisance because her family fulfilled his financial demands. But for Uthra's already burdened family, meeting the ever-increasing needs of Sooraj's family was proving to be impossible. The patience and the financial resources on both sides were running low. As far as Sooraj was concerned, Uthra had served her purpose. She was no longer of any monetary value to him and her presence in his home and in his life was an irritant at best.

There comes a time in some marriages when crossing the bridge to never return to the marital home becomes the only viable option for a partner. Sadly, Uthra's mental condition came in the way of such decision-making. Perhaps she envisaged a world with simpler people and most certainly with simpler outcomes, but burning bridges with her husband's family was far from her horizon of thought.

Sooraj, however, was different. He had a mind whose horizons stretched far beyond a simple separation. He wanted to avoid social ostracisation and also wanted to retain everything that he had unduly received from Uthra's family, down to the last penny. Having the best of both worlds comes at a huge price and unfortunately for Uthra, Sooraj was willing to pay it. He was willing to get rid of her!

February 2020

Sooraj was hooked to YouTube for long hours every day. He would often put off personal commitments and stay glued to his mobile phone. His entire search history was full of videos related to snakes. He wanted to learn every little detail about the snakes of Kerala and understand how serpents had made it to local folklore. His fetish for the reptile was clearly reaching obsessive limits.

This was the time when Sooraj first came across the exploits of Chavarukavu Suresh on his YouTube channel S.K. Media 2255. The first video he chanced upon was of Suresh expertly cornering a Russell's viper. The dexterity of Suresh's movements had Sooraj utterly spellbound. He was unable to peel his eyes off the tiny screen for several hours and ended up watching all the videos on the channel in a single session.

Sooraj did not sleep well that night. He kept imagining himself in place of the expert wrangler, capturing the deadliest of snakes. He was particularly fascinated by vipers and their ways. The sight of Suresh venturing into tight corners, evading the whiplike bite attempts by the snakes, and eventually holding them by their necks gave Sooraj an adrenaline rush. He also read the descriptions provided with every video and the entire comments section in detail. The virtual applause received by Suresh added to his feeling of excitement.

In his reading, Sooraj quickly deciphered that superstitious beliefs related to snakes were deeply rooted in the psyche of Keralites. Mythology said that Kerala was reclaimed from the waters of the Arabian Sea and given to the Nambudiris (a Malayali Brahmin clan) as a donation by Parashurama (one of the ten incarnations of the Hindu god Vishnu) to save himself from the sin of having killed numerous Kshatriya kings. Ancient Kerala was, however, full of forests and large tracts of its lands were ruled by the serpents. It was not fit for human habitation. Parashurama realised that co-habitation was the only way forward. He urged the people of the land to worship the serpents. Kerala had a small human population in those days and land holdings ran into several acres. It was customary for each family to reserve a certain portion of their land, typically one or two acres, for the snakes. These tracts were called *sarpakaavus* (snake groves).

Each snake grove had a shrine dedicated to snakes with one or more idols of the *naga raja* (the king of snakes) and other *naga devatas* (snake deities) inside. Snakes ruled these groves and people hardly ever ventured into them. The absence of human intervention ensured that the grove's ecosystem remained pristine—trees were never felled, bushes sprawled over, and vines grew eternally. The mythological stories attached to such groves fostered an amicable relationship between man and snake.

The premise of these snake groves was not based on benevolent divinity alone. There was a potent element of fear as well. Local communities believed that snakes, especially cobras, were manifestations of the divine. Harming snakes belonging to a grove was considered a sin that could invite a *sarpa dosha* (snake curse).

Sooraj realised that in this age-old belief was the scope of a cover-up. His mind was working on a devious plan which involved murder and he had zeroed in on his murder weapon. This weapon had a beating heart and a mind of its own.

The search for validation is intrinsic to human nature. For those in high-risk professions, this search is often more desperate. Ironically, the domain of these jobs comes with a lack of gratitude or praise. It is rare, for instance, for a common citizen to walk up to a man in a khaki uniform just to say a word of thanks. For a snake wrangler, such validation is rarer still. The professional wrangler is seen as a source of entertainment, not very different from a circus clown. Once the act is over and the curtains close, the fourth wall is never broken. The object of fascination is the catch, almost never the catcher.

It was the second week of February. The evening was balmy. Chavarukavu Suresh was comparing the fingers on his hands. The middle digit of his right hand looked visibly deformed. He began caressing it gently, wondering if the efforts he had put into capturing snakes over the years were worth all the pain. The damage on the finger made it look like a piece of absurdist art, as if it belonged in an artist's abstract depiction of war and certainly not on a human hand.

Suresh began to think of his daughter and wondered what would become of her if a venomous snake ever gave him a fatal bite in an effort to wriggle out. The financial returns from snake wrangling were small and any acknowledgement from society was negligible, if not altogether absent. His immense belief in his skill and the fact that he saw himself as a performing artist, a YouTube influencer of sorts, were what had kept him going. He shared the stage with a creature he found most fascinating and had deep respect for.

The sharp trilling of the famous Nokia ringtone broke Suresh's introspection. He stared down at his mobile phone which was beginning to give way. He had been saving money for the repair.

Suresh wanted to gather his thoughts before taking the call and answered it virtually on the last ring.

'Hello!' He sounded rather sombre.

'Sir, is this Chavarukavu Suresh?' An excited voice on the other end of the telephone line inquired.

'Yes, but I am not working today. Sorry!' Suresh decided to end the call brusquely.

'Sir! Sir, I am big fan!' Suresh heard only a faint version of this exclamation as he was removing the phone from his ear.

Hearing the word 'fan' was a first for Suresh, but it was exactly the kind of pat on the back that he needed given the disposition he found himself in. He decided to resume the conversation.

'Hello! Who is this?' he asked with the hint of a smile in his voice now.

'Sir, my name is Sooraj. I am an employee of HDFC Bank. I am a subscriber of your YouTube channel.'

'Thank you for your acknowledgment, Sooraj. What can I do for you?'

'Sir, I wanted to talk to you, my inspiration. I have been watching all your videos on a loop. I love snakes just like you do and your skills with a catching stick are simply mesmerising. You have changed my life, sir!'

Suresh did not know how to respond. The validation felt wonderful yet so foreign. He was used to cut-and-dried calls about where a snake had been spotted and how soon he could get there to catch it. There was a brief period of silence after which Sooraj spoke again.

'Sir, I want to learn from you. Do you mind if I occasionally exchange notes with you on snake wrangling?'

'No, I don't. Thank you for this call, Sooraj. You don't know how much I needed it,' Suresh said in a mellow tone.

'It is my pleasure. I will call again soon, sir!'

As Sooraj ended the call, he felt a sense of achievement. He had taken the first major step towards getting rid of Uthra. The soft corner he had already made for himself in Suresh's heart would serve him well.

Sooraj stayed true to his word and forged a friendly equation with Suresh in the week that followed their first telephonic conversation. He would frequently send messages to Suresh praising his work. He also made several inquiries about the snakes Suresh was handling. Suresh could make out that Sooraj's interest was not purely academic, but he was enjoying his day in the sun. He freely gave away information about the habitats of snakes, the properties of their venom, their fang types, etc. A typical conversation between the two men would read something like this:

'Which is your favourite snake?'

'How can I choose between my children? I respect them all.'

'That is why I am your fan, sir.'

'You are too kind.'

'Which one is the most venomous?'

'The cobra packs a serious punch. A single drop of its venom can account for several human lives.'

'What kind of venom does it possess?'

'The venom directly attacks the brain. The bites are often fatal.'

'Have you caught any recently?'

'Yes, I have.'

'Could you please forward some videos of the rescue to me? I am very keen to learn from your exemplary techniques.'

Suresh would often give in to these attempts at flattery and forward the videos he had with him. After a few days of similar conversations, Suresh agreed to meet Sooraj in person. The meeting was to take place on the banks of the Ithikkara River in Chathannoor.

Sooraj behaved every bit like a devoted fan around Suresh. He spoke at length about the latter's rescues and the exploits of Suresh's colleague Vava. He called himself a keen student of the art of wrangling and believed that in Suresh, he had found his mentor. He requested Suresh to continue teaching him about snakes and their ways. Before leaving, Sooraj pulled out a small *potli* (a small bundle) with *prasad* (blessed food) from the Sree Bhoothanatha Temple and offered it to Suresh. He said it was a form of *dakshina* (fees) for his guru.

Meeting someone who was a fan of his work had been a gratifying experience for Suresh. The world suddenly felt like an easier place to live in. After Sooraj had left, Suresh had stood by the river for a while and watched the sun go down. The orange hues of the sky with the coconut trees in the foreground looked beautiful. At one point, he felt like the shape of the trees' reflections in the water resembled the hood of a cobra.

The contact between Sooraj and Suresh remained constant for the next few weeks, and Sooraj soon acquired a considerable pool of knowledge about the snakes of Kerala. He could now pinpoint the venom glands on snakes, differentiate between venom types, and even vicariously understand what the scales on a snake's body would feel like. It was time now for the next step!

'How are you, Sooraj?' Suresh asked as he picked up the call on the first ring.

'I am doing well, sir. How are you?'

'I am fine too. Which serpent has robbed you of your sleep today?'

'Haha! Sir, I am actually calling with a proposal for you, something which will help the entire community where I live.'

'I am all ears.'

'Sir, we have many snakes in the neighbourhood, but the understanding that people have of the creatures is minimal. Everyone's first instinct is to kill the snake. I would like you to conduct a workshop to spread awareness about snakes and snake wranglers.'

'The idea sounds good, Sooraj, but will people be genuinely interested? Most of these workshops suffer from the problem of zero attendance.'

'Sir, leave that to me. I will ensure that there's a good crowd that gathers.'

Suresh paused for a bit. He knew that this was a chance for him to get some long overdue fame in the locality. 'I do not have a snake in my possession for a workshop right now. But I will get back to you as soon as I catch one,' he replied.

'Thank you, sir. I knew you would agree. I will eagerly wait for your next rescue.'

For once, Sooraj found himself in a situation where he had to wait for Suresh to make the next move. He was confident that he had inspired enough trust in the man for him to make that call, but the wait was agonising.

Sooraj was unusually irritable during this time, and Uthra was at the receiving end of a lot of his ire. Their infant son, Dhruv, was next in the line of fire. Uthra would often shield him the best she could, but she was finding it increasingly impossible to deal with Sooraj's changed disposition. However, she did not want to stir up another storm by getting her family involved.

She knew that they were already reeling under the pressure of her mother's chronic health issues.

Sooraj was doing some research while waiting for Suresh's call. He was scouring the internet for sedatives. He thought his plan of action would be more effective if the victim was knocked out. He wanted to get the balance just right because he also wanted to use the sedative on another person who would invariably be in his wife's room in the dark of night: his son Dhruv.

In the meantime, Suresh had landed a snake rescue mission for a female Russell's viper. The snake had been spotted near a building owned by the Oozhayikkodu Ayappa Temple Trust. The rescue was streamed live on Facebook and Sooraj was amongst those who were watching. This was a rather straightforward assignment for Suresh and he managed to capture the four-foot-long snake with ease. He carefully enclosed the snake in a plastic jar to complete the rescue.

Unable to control his excitement, Sooraj called Suresh soon after the rescue.

'Sir, I saw the live stream on your Facebook page. It was incredible.'

'Thank you, Sooraj. This was not a very complicated catch.'

'Sir, do you still have the snake?'

'Yes, I do. But I must relocate it soon.'

'Sir, can we use this snake for the awareness workshop?'

'Umm...I am not sure we should do that, Sooraj.'

'Sir, please think about it. The people here really need to learn about snakes, and I am willing to do anything for you to be able to conduct the workshop.'

'Then you will need to pay me for the workshop,' Suresh said jocularly.

'Just let me know the amount, sir!'

Sooraj's response was a surprise for Suresh. He had never thought that any financial gain would come from the workshop. While his initial demand had been made as a joke, his penury made him go down the road of exploiting Sooraj's desperation.

'Well, the workshop will cost Rs 10,000!' Suresh was ready to bargain.

'Okay, sir. I will arrange the money. Please make sure you get the highly poisonous snake with you,' Sooraj said excitedly.

'Yes, I will get the Russell's viper. What time should we fix for the workshop?'

'Sir, I think early morning will be ideal. I will make sure we have a decent attendance.'

As Suresh cut the phone, he could not believe his luck. Getting ten thousand for a workshop about snakes was absolutely unheard of. He quickly informed Raju, the driver of the rescue van, and Ligin and Premjith, the other rescuers he worked with, about the workshop and asked them to accompany him. A little later, Suresh received another call from Sooraj asking if he would be coming alone. For some reason, Suresh's gut instinct made him lie—he did not tell Sooraj about the little team he had assembled for the workshop.

Sooraj's mind was now in overdrive. He had managed to create the basic framework which would help him see the end of Uthra. His intentions were getting emboldened as he made progress in his alliance with Suresh. Sooraj had a world view which was completely dictated by moolah. The means did not matter, only the financial rewards did. The fact that he was willing to pay a hefty amount to Suresh just for conducting a workshop showed the extreme degree of his desperation because the one thing he never wished to part with was money.

Sooraj had a vivid imagination. He would often play through different scenarios of snake wrangling while watching Suresh's channel. This ability to visualise a snake wrangling situation had recently acquired a very sinister dimension. Sooraj would imagine himself tiptoeing into Uthra's room and letting loose a poisonous snake. Then he would think of possible reasons for the snake not biting his unsuspecting wife and rewind the reel. He would keep recalibrating his strategy each time he played out the whole scenario in his mind. He wanted the snake to represent the degree of brutality that existed in his thoughts. But he was slowly realising that his weapon of choice was a disciple of nature and was not as ruthless as he had envisaged it to be. Sooraj was learning that snakes have a complex brain and a clear idea of what they want to prey on.

Sooraj wished to get hold of the snake that Suresh was going to bring for the demonstration. He wanted to come up with a credible story to keep the snake in his possession after the workshop was done. In all his interactions with Suresh so far, he had noticed a few chinks in the man's armour—he was susceptible to flattery, he cared deeply for his daughter, and he was in need of money. Sooraj now began rehearsing a story built around all of these weaknesses to make sure that Suresh eventually gave in to his demand of handing over the Russell's viper to him. He was confident that he would be able to disarm Suresh by hook or by crook.

On the night before the workshop, Sooraj kept tossing and turning in his bed. He was too restless to even entertain the idea of sleep. Sometime after midnight, he got up and sat on the stairs outside the bedroom. He felt the adrenaline pumping through his veins. The play was about to begin and he had his characters lined up like puppets on strings. He could not wait for daybreak. Every now and then, he kept checking whether his phone was charged or not. At one point in time during the night, he went and picked up his son from his crib which was placed next to Uthra. He stared at the baby's face with a look that could only be described as lovingly evil. He knew that he was about to turn the little boy's life upside down, but he also saw the absolute necessity of doing what he was going to do.

Hours later, when the clock struck five and day broke, Sooraj felt a hollow in his stomach. He had spent the better part of the night pacing up and down the stairs after putting his son back in the crib, but now, the time to receive his mentor had finally arrived.

27 February 2020

Sooraj hopped onto his bicycle. It was a pleasant morning and the gushing wind added a rhythmic beat to the pounding of his heart. As he pedalled along, he felt a sense of strength. He looked up at the sun as it gained prominence and felt like it was his pedalling that was responsible for it.

When he reached the Karakkadu junction a little later, he parked his cycle next to the road and waited for Suresh to come. After a short while, Suresh reached the spot in his rescue van.

But Sooraj was totally unnerved when he saw other people inside the van with Suresh. He could feel his plans slip away as Suresh got down from the van and walked towards him. When they embraced each other in greeting, it was a cold embrace.

'Good morning, Sooraj! I hope everything is okay?' Suresh began on a note of concern after sensing a lack of Sooraj's usual warmth.

'Yes, sir. All is well!' Sooraj sounded slightly frazzled even as he hastened to assure Suresh.

The three men accompanying Suresh now stepped out of the van. Sooraj looked at them with a gaze that instantly made all of them feel out of place.

'Meet my associates Raju, Ligin, and Premjith. They are all excited about the workshop and will help me in the demonstration today.' Suresh tried to bring some ease into the proceedings.

'Sir, do you have the snake?' Sooraj inquired.

'Yes, Sooraj. The snake is safe in a jar.' Suresh could now sense the urgency in Sooraj's demeanour.

Sooraj knew that he needed to collect himself. The presence of the three extra men was an unforeseen and unwanted development, but he still wanted to continue with his larger plan. He took a few deep steadying breaths and looked towards Suresh's associates with a reassuring smile.

'Thank you so much for coming. I am so happy to host you all. It will be an honour to watch my hero and his friends in action.' Sooraj had regained some of his mojo. 'Let us walk towards my place. We have to do the demonstration in my locality.'

Suresh took the jar which contained the captive snake and some other equipment out of the van. Raju checked if there were other things that they may be forgetting to take along with them before locking up the van. In the meantime, Sooraj made small talk with Premjith and Ligin.

Sooraj's original plan had been to keep the snake after Suresh's workshop. He was mentally armed to lower Suresh's defences and had even thought of an opening line highlighting both his daughter's future and his penury. However, the presence of Suresh's associates had now made this process tricky. He did not want to create a trail of witnesses who could cause him trouble if things were to go south. As they began the walk towards Sooraj's locality, he began to think of possible improvisations in his strategy. Suddenly, he stopped under an electric pole and turned to Suresh.

'Sir, do you have any more snakes in the car?' he asked.

'Yes, there are some non-venomous snakes in other jars inside the van.'

'Hmm, okay. Sir, I would recommend that all of you have some tea at the shop next to the bus stop ahead. It is quite a famous tea stall here. In the meantime, I will go home and prepare everything for the workshop.'

As Sooraj looked at Suresh and waited for a response, he could see that this change of course had put him off a little. He quickly took Suresh aside and handed over the promised Rs 10,000 to him. He also requested Suresh to give him the jar containing the Russell's viper. Unable to resist the money in front of him, Suresh agreed to hand over the jar and head to the bus stop with his associates.

'If anyone asks why you are here, tell them that you heard a Russell's viper has been spotted in the locality and that you are here to catch it,' were Sooraj's parting words.

Suresh next heard from Sooraj a little while later at about seven in the morning.

'I hope the tea lived up to the hype?' Sooraj chuckled.

'Yes, it was full of spices. Premjith particularly enjoyed it!'

'That's great. Anyway, you can come to my locality now. I have assembled a decent-sized crowd. Please come in the rescue van as it has the other snakes. And as I requested, tell the people that you are here to catch a Russell's viper.'

By now Suresh could sense that Sooraj had no intention of returning the Russell's viper that he had handed over to him earlier. The money that Sooraj had given him was meant for the snake, not the demonstration he was about to conduct. However, he wanted his share of fame too and decided to ignore the danger that lay in Sooraj gaining custody of the venomous snake. He also saw an opportunity for making more money in the future.

When Suresh and his associates reached Sooraj's house, they found quite a few people already gathered there. In front of the onlookers, Sooraj then asked them to conduct a thorough search of the premises. He wanted them to look for a Russell's viper. But no matter how hard they looked, no snake was found.

Some people asked Suresh about his presence in the locality. He stuck to Sooraj's version and said, 'I am here because I received an anonymous tip that a Russell's viper was seen here. Unfortunately, we haven't been able to spot it.'

Sooraj soon gathered the onlookers and proposed the idea for a demonstration. He said that the rare opportunity of having an expert snake wrangler in their midst should not be wasted. 'Sir, we request you to conduct an awareness workshop for us. The people of our locality will be very grateful to you and your team.' Sooraj wore a look of absolute innocence as he spoke to Suresh.

'Yes, I will certainly conduct a demonstration. I am in this profession to help people after all.' Suresh also wanted to make the most of his moment in the sun.

This was met with a round of applause by a crowd that was growing in size by the minute. Ligin, Premjith, and Raju were also enjoying the attention.

'Let me get a snake from the rescue van so that we can hold the demonstration,' Suresh announced, and came back with a snake in a couple of minutes.

The demonstration started soon after. Suresh charmed the crowd with his incredible skill. He showed them the use of snake sticks and tongs like a true artist. His movements were measured and had a certain feline grace to them. The audience watched the proceedings with rapt attention. Sooraj's family was also among the attendees of the demonstration. The entire workshop was being filmed by Premjith.

During the demonstration, Suresh asked for an audience member to volunteer. Sooraj's hand went up immediately. Suresh handed a snake tong to Sooraj and asked him to try and catch the snake while he had the reptile secured from the tail end.

Suresh was used to seeing people pale with fear in these circumstances. However, Sooraj was eerily confident. It was as if he had run through this scenario a hundred times. He handled the snake deftly and eventually decided to do a solo show of his own. There was a rousing round of applause for Sooraj's efforts.

The crowd cleared soon after the demonstration was over and Suresh's associates took their seats in the van. Suresh placed the snake he had used for the demonstration back in a jar and handed it over to Premjith.

Sooraj then took Suresh aside for a conversation.

'Thank you, sir. The demonstration was a huge success,' he said and shook Suresh's hand.

'I should be the one thanking you. This was a high point in my career!' Suresh did not sound like his usual self.

Sensing the uneasiness in Suresh's body language, Sooraj tried to douse the flames of suspicion in his mind and offered him an explanation. 'I know you must be wondering about what happened to the Russell's viper. Actually, my family is into farming, and there is an infestation of large rats in our fields that we've been dealing with. That is why I need the snake.'

'Okay. I understand,' Suresh responded. He did not want to pursue the matter further, lest it harm the business potential of his equation with Sooraj.

Their parting was just as cold as their meeting had been.

On the way back to Chathannoor, Suresh paid some money to each of his associates.

Sooraj was a believer in dumb luck. While he knew that snakes like the Russell's viper need grave provocation to bite a human being, he decided to still go ahead and put his luck to the test. On the same evening as the demonstration, he kept the viper on the staircase that led to Uthra's bedroom and then sent Uthra upstairs to fetch his mobile phone. He was hopeful that the viper would deliver a fatal bite as Uthra went past it. Unfortunately for him, Uthra saw the snake on her way up the stairs and shrieked. Not wanting others to get involved, Sooraj emerged as the knight in shining armour and skilfully captured the viper. He put it inside a sack and kept it aside after securing its opening. He then hugged Uthra, expressing a fake sense of relief over her close escape. Since a snake rescuer had visited their place on the day of the incident, Uthra believed Sooraj when he said that it was a rat snake meant specifically for the workshop that the rescuer had hosted.

A few days later, Manimekhala visited Uthra to ask after her well-being. Uthra told her mother about the incident involving the snake on the staircase. She also told her about how Sooraj had rushed to her rescue, caught the snake, and placed it in a sack which he luckily had handy. This episode sounded of little significance to Manimekhala and she soon changed the course of the conversation. Her primary motive was to save her daughter's marriage, and the presence of a snake on the landing of a staircase was the least of her concerns.

In the wake of his failed first attempt, Sooraj spent several sleepless nights cursing himself for acting like an impatient rookie. He knew that even a single thread of suspicion could mar this entire exercise and he could ill-afford that. Time was quickly running out and he had to act fast.

For a couple of days after the workshop, there was radio silence between mentor and mentee. Suresh was concerned. He was used to Sooraj being in touch with him almost on a daily basis. On the third day, Suresh decided to drop Sooraj a greeting by sending him the picture of a beautiful landscape that featured coconut trees. There was, however, no response from Sooraj. Worry began to gnaw at Suresh now. Was his golden goose slipping away from him?

When days turned into a week, Suresh sent some fresh videos of snake wrangling to Sooraj. One of the videos featured the daring rescue of a cobra that had slithered its way onto the top shelf of a makeshift cupboard in someone's house. But even these videos which were tailor-made for a snake enthusiast like Sooraj were met with silence. Suresh now understood that something was cooking, but he was unaware of just how sinister Sooraj's intentions were. After that, every now and then, his mind would go back to the Russell's viper that he had sold to Sooraj.

For Sooraj, Suresh's messages were a nuisance now. He had even silenced his message notification ringtone. His mind was a case study straight out of a *Criminology 101* textbook—once a person has lost his or her utility, they are to be discarded ruthlessly. There was no genuine emotion involved and everything said in the process of getting to know a person was just for effect. Sooraj's supposed respect for Suresh had evaporated as soon as the real crime was on the boil. His focus was now squarely on snuffing out a life.

He had his murder weapon. He was also carefully calibrating the concoction of sleeping pills he would have to administer by testing them out on his unsuspecting wife. Uthra would invariably wake up with a headache every morning, but she did not think much of this development. She attributed it simply to fatigue.

A CAUSE TOO DEAR

2 March 2020

It was well past midnight when Uthra woke up with excruciating pain in her right leg and began to wail loudly.

Her cries for help were a major setback for Sooraj. His sedative mixture had clearly not proved potent enough and Uthra had woken up before the hemotoxic venom of the Russell's viper could completely overpower her body.

Knowing that he would eventually have to respond, Sooraj leapt out of bed and rushed to Uthra's aid. For a couple of minutes though, he acted as if he was not able to make sense of the situation. Uthra kept telling him that she had been bitten by something. Sooraj told Uthra that he was going to call for help, but instead, he bided his time.

When it soon became evident that prolonging Uthra's desperate need for first aid was not going to be enough to silence her forever, Sooraj called his friend Sujith at nearly three in the morning. The first call went unanswered and Sooraj breathed a sigh of relief. Somewhere at the back of his devious mind he registered that he had created an alibi of sorts. His parents were at home too, and Sooraj knew how to drive. He could have sought their help and driven Uthra to the hospital himself. But he consciously decided to do neither.

Just as Sooraj was growing used to Uthra's cries for help, Sujith called back.

'Sooraj! Why did you call me at this hour? I hope everything is okay?' Sujith's concern was evident.

'No, Sujith! Uthra has been bitten by something and she's in great pain. I think she needs to go to the hospital.'

'You must rush her to the government hospital! I will see you there!'

'I was hoping you could pick us up, Sujith!'

'Oh okay. I will be there as soon as possible.'

Sujith's residence was barely two kilometres away and he managed to make it to Sree Surya in five minutes. He found Sooraj's mother waiting on the ground floor, and she informed him that the couple was still in the bedroom upstairs. Sujith ran up the stairs in a jiffy and found Uthra crying in extreme pain. He glanced at Sooraj who looked surprisingly unperturbed. Without wasting anymore time, he asked Sooraj to help him carry Uthra to his car, and seeing no way out of the situation he was embroiled in, Sooraj acceded to the request.

'How did this happen?' Sujith asked Sooraj while driving as fast as he could to the hospital.

'We had gone to the Ezhamkulam Devi Temple in connection with the Kumbha Bharani[7] festival and got back

---

7 The festival is held as a thanksgiving to Goddess Bhadrakali for a rich harvest and for protection from diseases and calamities.

home around 8.30 p.m. We walked along the paddy fields. After we got back home, I went out again with some friends and returned by 10 p.m. I also had a couple of drinks with my father. When I entered our bedroom, Uthra told me that she had gone out of the house to wash some clothes when something bit her. She said she had fallen to the ground after that and had had a terrible headache since then. She took a Sibelium tablet for the headache and went to sleep. And then, in the middle of the night, I was woken up by her cries for help. That is when I called you.' Sooraj had rattled off the entire chain of events with little emotion.

Sujith had a lot of questions on his mind, but he knew that at that point in time, the priority was to get medical help for Uthra. With every passing second, he could see that she was becoming increasingly giddy. He rushed the couple to the government hospital in Adoor where they were received by a nurse on emergency duty. She quickly assessed that Uthra was in deep distress and called for the doctor.

When Dr Jariya Haneef got there shortly, she carefully examined the bite wound.

'When was she bitten?' She looked at Sooraj.

'Around nine perhaps. She had gone out of the house for some work.'

'How are you related to the patient?'

'I am her husband.'

All this while, Uthra had been clutching her right leg and crying incessantly. Dr Haneef now turned her attention towards her.

'What is your name?'

Uthra almost screamed out her name in pain.

'Did you see what bit you?' the doctor asked while studying the bite wound which lay between Uthra's ankle and her knee.

'No. I have no idea.'

'Why did you not bring her to the hospital as soon as she was bitten?' the doctor asked Sooraj.

Sooraj mumbled something in response and gave no definitive answer.

Dr Haneef immediately got down to the protocol that is generally employed in cases of bites of unknown origin. She administered Avil[8] and Efcorlin[9] injections to Uthra. She also sent a sample of Uthra's blood to the lab and asked for the clotting time to be observed.

'Seven minutes,' the technician informed Dr Haneef a little later.

The result indicated a high possibility of a hemotoxic snakebite. Dr Haneef felt that the hospital was ill-equipped in the absence of a physician to deal with the situation. She also decided to forego the ELISA test[10] in the interest of saving critical time and referred Uthra to the Holy Cross Hospital.

By this time, it was quarter to four in the morning. Dr Chaithanya Sidhartha was working as the casualty medical officer at the Holy Cross Hospital when Uthra was helped into the ward by Sujith and Sooraj. The reference issued by the government hospital spoke of an unknown bite sustained around

---

8 Avil is an anti-allergic medication.

9 Efcorlin has anti-inflammatory and immunosuppressant properties.

10 ELISA stands for enzyme linked-immunoassay. It is a standard test used for the clinical diagnosis of snakebite.

nine at night but indicated a high possibility of the presence of a hemotoxic venom. Uthra was drowsy and unable to make sense of anything being said to her. She was writhing and kicking her legs in excruciating pain.

Sidhartha checked Uthra's vitals and found her blood pressure to be dangerously low. He immediately asked the nurse on duty to get her started on intravenous fluids and made a quick assessment of the resources available. The bite mark on Uthra's right leg was oozing blood, and her pain was through the charts. She could almost feel her tissues fall apart one at a time. The intravenous (IV) fluids that were being pumped into her system were not proving to be effective either. Unfortunately, the doctor could not have administered any anti-venom until Uthra's vitals stabilised. Dr Sidhartha realised that another referral to a higher medical centre was required. The absence of ventilator support at Holy Cross was the primary basis of his decision. He asked for the high-tech ambulance to be pressed into service and referred Uthra to the Pushpagiri Medical College Hospital in Tiruvalla.

Anuraj, the emergency medical technician at Holy Cross Hospital, accompanied Sooraj and Sujith in the ambulance as they took Uthra to the next hospital. Uthra began slipping in and out of consciousness on the way, but there was no change in Sooraj's calm demeanour over the obvious deterioration in his wife's condition.

Sooraj's sister called Syamdev, Uthra's cousin, at three in the morning to inform him about what had transpired. His phone, however, went unanswered; it was probably on silent mode. A little later, she called Syamdev's father and informed him about Uthra's condition.

'Syam! Syam!'

Syamdev sprang up from his slumber when he heard his father call out his name so frantically. 'Papa! What happened?'

'Uthra has been bitten by something and she has been rendered unconscious. Please come quickly.'

Syamdev immediately called Sooraj. But Sooraj did not answer his call. Next, he placed a call to Uthra's father and shared with him the sketchy details that had come through via Sooraj's sister. He promised to pick him up shortly and take him to Sooraj's house. A little later, while they were on their way to Sree Surya, both Syamdev and Vijayasenan tried to call Sooraj several times but he did not answer their calls. On reaching Sree Surya, they were informed by Sooraj's family that Uthra had been referred to the Pushpagiri Medical College Hospital in Tiruvalla. Without wasting a minute, they immediately left for Tiruvalla and caught up with the ambulance carrying Uthra.

Dr Bhuvaneswari was the post-graduate resident doctor on duty in the Emergency Medicine Department at Pushpagiri Medical College Hospital. At around 4.50 a.m., Uthra was rolled into the emergency ward on a stretcher. Bhuvaneswari made a quick preliminary assessment of Uthra's condition. She placed Uthra's age at around twenty-five, and saw that her vitals were sinking by the second. The referral notes from the local hospital cited elevated clotting time. Her triage[11] indicated priority one. Uthra was still conscious, but she wore a look of listlessness. Medically, her condition could be summed up as being unstable! Uthra was once again hooked to an IV drip. The doctor also asked the nurse to conduct another clotting test. Then Bhuvaneswari went to get Uthra's treatment summary from Sooraj.

'What time was she bitten?'

'Around nine in the night.'

'Why did you ignore her complaints?'

Once again Sooraj kept mum.

'What took you so long?' The doctor sounded irritated now.

'There was a delay in arranging transport.' Sooraj looked sheepish.

Sensing that the husband was not going to be forthcoming with information, Bhuvaneswari scurried back to her wailing patient.

'More than twenty minutes!' the nurse exclaimed on seeing the result of the clotting test.

Bhuvaneswari knew that administering an anti-venom with Uthra's unstable condition could lead to severe complications, but not doing so was tantamount to awarding a death sentence to the patient.

'Give her ten vials of polyvalent anti-venom.[12] We are

---

[11] The preliminary assessment of patients or casualties that is done in order to determine the urgency of their need for treatment and the nature of treatment required. The triage scale consists of three categories: one (immediate), two (urgent), and three (non-urgent).

[12] An anti-venom that is effective against multiple species.

running out of time,' Bhuvaneswari instructed the nurse who immediately complied.

While the anti-venom was being administered, Bhuvaneswari did a close inspection of the wound on Uthra's right leg. It was roughly twenty centimetres above the ankle and was still bleeding. She also took pictures of the wound with her mobile phone's camera.

A little later, Uthra's vitals began to stabilise. The doctor passed on this news to the family, and there was tangible relief on Vijayasenan and Syamdev's faces. Bhuvaneswari warned them about the risks Uthra faced after being given the anti-venom. She also informed them that her road to recovery was going to be long and strenuous.

The family's relief, however, was short-lived. At 6.30 a.m., Uthra's vitals began to fluctuate again. Her blood pressure fell so low that it was no longer recordable. She was started on a noradrenaline infusion and her BP improved to 90/60. But this episode prompted the medicos in charge of Uthra's case to shift her to the Critical Care department that was headed by Dr Mathew Pulikkan.

It took a few days for Uthra's vitals to stabilise, after which she was shifted to the Department of Plastic Surgery on 6 March. The doctors there found a lot of dead muscle around the bite wound and performed a debridement surgery[13] for its removal on 7 March. All the anterior compartment muscles of the right leg meant for backward movement of the ankle and extension of the toes were removed as well. After that, Uthra

[13] An invasive procedure to remove dead or infected tissue.

had further surgeries on 11 and 23 March, and then again on 15 April. Before her discharge on 22 April, Uthra also had to undergo a skin grafting operation.

Uthra's treatment lasted all of fifty-two days. She was non-ambulant at the time of her discharge. She was not prescribed any medicines, but her wound needed dressing twice a week for which she had to visit the hospital. Uthra expressed a desire to go to her parents' house after she was discharged and her wishes were honoured. Vijayasenan had borne the entire bill of Rs 10 lakh for Uthra's treatment. This was another major blow to the assets of an already overburdened family.

Criminal intent sometimes supersedes all notions of logic. The insatiability of some criminal minds only ends after committing the final act. Sooraj was caught in a similar infinite loop of bloodlust. There is no better deterrent for a prospective murderer than a failed attempt, but Sooraj was living in an exclusively evil space of mind. His wife, Uthra, was the clearly identifiable victim of his rage and he would stop at nothing!

Experienced policemen who profile criminal minds note that the cold-blooded intent to murder someone at all costs is usually aimed at a person whom the criminal knows intimately. Terms like hate, revenge, and justice acquire much graver motives when they squeeze into a vacuum previously occupied by love. In this particular case, a cocktail of reasons had painted the target in bold red on Uthra's back, but exactly what moment or what reason had made Sooraj snap would be, as it was with a lot of other criminal impulses, left to the imagination.

The wide reach of American culture has taught us quite a few things. One which ardent followers of American crime dramas will connect with is the idea of murder in the first degree. The three components that comprise such a murder are wilfulness, deliberation, and premeditation. Such a murder also carries the highest of penalties for its obvious cold-bloodedness.

Wilfulness is directly linked with purpose. It needs to be clearly established that the intention was indeed to kill. Deliberation refers to going ahead with the kill in spite of knowing the consequences that the offence may lead to. Premeditation is the act of carefully planning the murder before committing it.

Sooraj was now treating his first attempt on Uthra's life like a net practice session before a grand finale. He was recalibrating every aspect of his approach to the crime. There was a lot to consider: the inherent resistance of the victim, the availability of first responders, and the potency of the murder weapon. Unfortunately for Uthra, the attempt had failed because of factors that fell squarely within Sooraj's control. Her life was in imminent danger and the person she would trust with her life was the primary cause of this peril.

UNTIL DEATH DO US PART

7 May 2020

An otherwise normal morning was torn apart by Manimekhala's shrieks. Vijayasenan dropped the newspaper he was reading and forced his ageing legs up the stairs and into Uthra's room. Vishu, Uthra's brother, followed his father. The two men saw Uthra lying in a supine position with her mouth open and her left hand hanging out of the cot. Manimekhala was sitting next to her daughter in a resigned posture.

'What happened?' Vijaysenan's voice quivered with fear.

'She is not responding. I have tried shaking her, but she is just lying there, lifeless.'

Amidst all the commotion, Sooraj, who had come to stay with Uthra at her parents' place only the previous evening, also entered the room.

'We must rush her to the hospital!' Vishu announced and immediately took charge of the situation. He quickly picked up Uthra and carried her down the stairs towards the car shed. On the way down, he noticed that there was a bite mark on her left arm. He handed Sooraj the keys to the car, but Sooraj was reluctant to drive. Vishu hurriedly put Uthra in the backseat and drove the family to St. Joseph's Mission Hospital in Anchal.

'Madam, please come fast. The patient has no vitals!' a paramedic exclaimed after Uthra was rushed into the emergency ward.

Dr Jeena Badhar immediately rushed to the observation room where Uthra was lying motionless on a stretcher. Since COVID protocols were being observed, only Sooraj had been allowed inside the room. The others were nervously waiting in the adjoining corridor outside.

'Something has bitten her on the left arm.' Sooraj put on an act of concern.

'Who are you?' the doctor asked.

'I am her husband.'

'It looks like a snakebite. You must search your home for the snake. I will examine her in the meantime,' Dr Badhar said while observing the clotting on Uthra's arm.

As the doctor got down to work, Sooraj left the room and informed his in-laws that Uthra had, according to the doctor, probably been bitten by a snake. He told Vishu that they would have to search the house for a snake as instructed by the doctor. Right after that, they left to look for the snake, leaving Uthra's worried parents at the hospital.

Back inside the examination room, Dr Badhar had made several observations—Uthra's pupils were dilated, her extremities were cold, she did not have a pulse, and her blood pressure was not recordable. She wiped the blood off Uthra's left arm with an alcohol swab. Four bite marks were clearly visible on the arm. Dr Badhar then conducted an ECG examination on Uthra and came to the gravest conclusion: Uthra was no more.

Dr Badhar stepped out into the corridor adjoining the observation room and asked for someone from the patient's family. When Uthra's mother came up to her, she told her about her daughter's death. Manimekhala broke down as she heard the news that is any parent's worst nightmare. She looked towards her husband who was seated a little distance away and was looking at her expectantly. But one look at Manimekhala confirmed Vijayasenan's fear too. He began sobbing as soon as their eyes met. For the purpose of declaring Uthra's death officially, Manimekhala was asked to go into the observation room. If hearing the news of her daughter's death was hard, then seeing her child lying lifelessly on the stretcher was harder still, and Manimekhala began wailing loudly.

Dr Badhar gave Manimekhala a few moments to gather herself and then she asked her, 'Please tell me, how did this happen?'

'She was at home with us, recovering from one snakebite and now this…' Manimekhala sounded shattered.

'She's been bitten by a snake before?'

'Yes, she recently received treatment for a snakebite.'

The doctor found this extremely suspicious and advised Uthra's mother that a post-mortem examination be conducted on Uthra's body.

In the meantime, Vijayasenan received a call from Sooraj.

'We have managed to kill the snake. It was hiding under the cupboard in the dressing room. Some kerosene and a stick did the trick.' Sooraj sounded rather excited, given the sombre circumstances.

'She is gone, Sooraj. Hurry and come to the hospital now,' Vijayasenan mumbled with what felt like the last ounce of energy left in his body.

On receiving the news, Sooraj and Vishu immediately left for the hospital. During the drive to the hospital, Sooraj managed to assume an outer facade of devastation while a sense of achievement was surging within. He was also thinking about where he could bury the dead snake upon his return from the hospital.

A little later, the doctor called Vijayasenan into the observation room. She asked him to find out which snake had bitten Uthra; she needed that piece of information for the purpose of creating a detailed case summary. Vijayasenan called Sooraj.

'Which snake was it?'

'It was a cobra.' Sooraj sounded reasonably confident in his answer.

Soon, Dr Badhar made an entry in the register where a record of all those who were declared 'brought dead' to the hospital was kept. Even though she had filled in the names of patients in the past, every case brought with it a little heartbreak. She made a note of the details of Uthra's case in her beautiful handwriting and referred the body for a post-mortem examination.

When Sooraj and Vishu finally reached the hospital a little while later, they were greeted by a devastated Vijayasenan and Manimekhala. The old man hugged Vishu and cried for a while. Sooraj headed towards the observation room to understand what was being done to Uthra's body.

Vishu had, by now, become suspicious of the circumstances surrounding Uthra's death and he decided to lodge a complaint with the police. His First Information Statement (FIS) was recorded by Grade Sub-Inspector J. Joy at around 11.30 a.m. in the Anchal police station on the same day as Uthra's death. In the meantime, Sooraj had managed to go back to Uthra's house and bury the snake.

After the necessary samples were collected for a post-mortem examination, Uthra was cremated the same evening in the presence of close relatives and friends. A police constable was also on duty at the cremation site.

Soon after the cremation, Sooraj approached Vijayasenan. An air of grief and fatigue hung heavy around the old man.

'What will happen to Dhruv now?' Sooraj sobbed.

'We are all going to take care of him,' Vijayasenan assured his son-in-law.

'Yes, but I am his father. He will be in my care.'

Vijayasenan had a lot to say to Sooraj, but against the background of the heavy loss he had just suffered, all he could manage at that point in time was a half nod.

'You are aware of my circumstances. Raising Dhruv alone will be difficult. You must continue giving me financial aid,' Sooraj continued with a reasonable degree of composure.

Shocked, Vijayasenan could only stare back at him and maintained an indefinite silence this time.

8 May 2020

A distraught Vijayasenan began running through the chain of events that had led to Uthra's demise. The demand for money from Sooraj immediately after the cremation had pushed his mind into a restless state. He also recalled that Sooraj had been awake much earlier than usual the previous morning. In fact, Sooraj had washed a glass tumbler in the sink while Vijayasenan was making his morning tea. He now decided to ask Sooraj a few probing questions.

'I can't believe we have been struck by this tragedy,' he began.

Sooraj nodded.

'Was the window in the room open?'

'Yes. But I closed it late at night,' Sooraj replied.

Vijayasenan immediately knew that this submission by Sooraj was false. His wife used to clean Uthra's room with an antiseptic solution every night and she always made sure that the window was shut.

'So you think the serpent entered the room through the window?'

'Yes. I knew something like this could happen. Uthra was a victim of sarpa dosha.'

The fact that Sooraj was trying to blame everything on the supernatural made Vijayasenan even more suspicious. He decided to discontinue the conversation for the time being and consult Manimekhala about his doubts.

Meanwhile, Manimekhala had been staring at one of Uthra's portraits since morning. She had not yet found the courage to make it out of bed. She was crying intermittently and blaming herself for what had happened to her daughter.

Like her husband, she had also been running through the events that had led to Uthra's death, especially the evening of 6 May, and she had grown suspicious of Sooraj and his intentions. When Sooraj had appeared at their residence that evening, it was an unexpected arrival. Then at night, when he had requested her for a glass of juice which he wanted to give to Uthra, it had been a surprise for Manimekhala because she had served Uthra some juice only a little while earlier. However, Sooraj had been insistent and had promised her that it was really Uthra who wanted to drink the juice. Sometime after that, he had gone out of the house through the kitchen door and returned with a black shoulder bag a little while later. After dinner, when Manimekhala had gone to disinfect Uthra's room, she had noticed that the glass with the juice was still untouched. She had cleaned her daughter's room as usual and had made sure that the window was closed before leaving the room. Sooraj had bolted the door from the inside after she left. Manimekhala had returned to her room and had browsed through some things on her mobile phone until midnight, after which she had gone to sleep.

Now, just as she was reaching out for Uthra's wedding album to flip through some pictures and relive some old memories, Vijayasenan entered the room. He told his wife about Sooraj's fidgety behaviour when confronted about the sequence of events on the day of Uthra's demise. Manimekhala shared Vijayasenan's doubts in full and added a few observations of her own. They decided to confront Sooraj and his family, and surmised that the best way to do so would be to talk about the heavy loans that Sooraj had taken from them.

Later that evening, the grieving parents called Syamdev over. They asked him to take the lead in talking to Sooraj since he shared the closest equation with him. Syamdev was also desperate to get justice for the family and he immediately agreed to the proposal. He went and initiated a conversation with Sooraj.

'Sooraj, how are you doing?' he asked.

'I am trying to keep my emotions in check. It is a difficult time.'

'I understand. I was talking to Uthra's parents today. They are in great financial difficulty after having shouldered the entire weight of the expenditure at Pushpagiri.'

'Hmm. But they have enough,' Sooraj countered Syamdev.

'Actually, they don't. You must assure them that you will create a corpus for Dhruv's future.'

'But I don't have anything!' Sooraj exclaimed.

'You still have Uthra's gold ornaments and the car her parents gave you. You can sell all of it and use the money to ensure that Dhruv gets a good education.'

'I don't think that is a good idea.' Sooraj's tenor changed as soon as he saw that the conversation was beginning to wade into the waters of the dowry he had received.

'I do not think you have an option, Sooraj. You must fulfil the responsibility of being a father and a son-in-law.'

'I have no such responsibility. In fact, Vijayasenan should keep sending me money every month so that I can look after Dhruv.'

'Don't be ridiculous, Sooraj!' Syamdev exclaimed, unable to believe what he was hearing.

'Let us not discuss this matter any further,' Sooraj said firmly and moved away, bringing the conversation to an end.

9 May 2020

The next day, Syamdev urged Sooraj to pick up the threads of the conversation that had abruptly ended the previous day. Sooraj was already irked after the routine interrogation he had undergone at the Anchal police station as a follow-up to the FIS that Vishu had lodged.

'Look...Syamdev, I am not going to sell the car or the gold. In fact, I think that the property that is in Uthra's name should be sold and the money should be transferred to me. If not, then the property should be transferred to Dhruv's name.'

'This is preposterous. Do you realise you are talking about further burdening Uthra's parents?'

'I am just talking about safeguarding Dhruv's future.'

Syamdev couldn't digest what he was hearing and he stormed off.

14 May 2020

The next set of verbal volleys was exchanged when Sooraj's mother was also present. Uthra's parents made it clear that they wanted the assets which Sooraj had received by way of dowry to be liquefied and transferred to a fixed deposit. This suggestion was met with the most dramatic reaction by Sooraj's mother. She declared that even death does not take away a woman's love for her gold ornaments. Then she pushed Dhruv to the ground and fainted herself. Sooraj ran to her and picked her up, and before anyone could make sense of what was happening, he rushed her to the Anchal Mission Hospital.

A little later, the police arrived at Uthra's parents' house and told Vijayasenan that Sooraj's sister had filed a complaint against his family for assaulting her mother and brother. This development removed any lingering shreds of empathy that Vijaysenan might have had for Sooraj and his family.

Vijayasenan and Manimekhala were now convinced that Sooraj had murdered their daughter. Everything they had witnessed after Uthra's passing had confirmed that it was Sooraj's greed and not a divine sarpa dosha that could account for their daughter's death. They decided to submit an application to the superintendent of police asking for expedient action. They laid the blame squarely on Sooraj's doorstep.

'Why have you not filed a complaint against Sooraj so far?' the SP inquired.

'Sir, we wanted to avoid acting out of any prejudice against our son-in-law. But this bogus complaint by his sister has removed any doubts that we had about the right course of action. We now want the police to get to the bottom of the matter.'

'Okay. I understand now why the FIS does not name Sooraj as the accused. I will instruct the concerned police station to provide you with complete assistance.'

Vijayasenan and Manimekhala had found a purpose to live after their daughter's demise. They were determined to get her justice!

DIAL 100

7 May 2020

The day would have gone by in a largely uneventful manner at the police station in Anchal had it not been for the angry outburst of Inspector Gopal Nair, the embattled SHO, in the morning. His anger was arising out of the frustration he felt for not being able to control the upward trend of crime in his jurisdiction. The officers working under him had all been told to pull up their socks in no uncertain terms.

The news of the murder of a young woman was the last thing the SHO was mentally prepared to receive. When he had arrived at the police station that morning, he had found a young man sobbing uncontrollably as he reported his suspicions about the death of his sister.

'How was your sister killed? What is the weapon the killer used to kill her? Are you sure she did not die of natural causes?' Nair asked a volley of questions.

'Sir, she was bitten by a snake,' Vishu replied.

'Then how is it a murder? Snakebites often lead to death,' Nair dismissed Vishu's response.

'I know, sir, but in this case, there are many reasons why I suspect foul play.'

Not really convinced, Nair instructed the police station clerk to tend to Vishu and left for another crime scene.

In instances of the death of a woman due to an unnatural cause within seven years of marriage and where a relative expresses apprehension and suspects foul play, an FIR has to be registered as prescribed under Section 174 of the Criminal Procedure Code. And so it was in the case of Uthra's death as well. On the basis of what Vishu told the police, a case was registered, and the body was duly despatched for a post-mortem examination after the preparation of an inquest report[14] by GSI Joy. This exercise had consumed most of the day.

Meanwhile, in the same police station, Sub Inspector (SI) Pushpkumar was rushing through the writing of a case diary as the investigation deadline was close. He was also hoping to find enough time after the completion of the investigation to go to the Ithikkara River, which flowed through the northern side of the police station's jurisdiction and demarcated its border with the Kadakkal police station, and take a refreshing dip in its cool waters. This was something he habitually did when he thought his day's work had earned him a few stolen moments of relaxation.

---

[14] In preparing an inquest report, the inquiring officer describes the apparent cause of death, including details about such wounds, fractures, bruises, and other marks of injury as may be found on the body, and stating in what manner, or by what weapon or instrument (if any) such injuries appear to have been inflicted.

When Pushpkumar went to the head constable manning the station's clerical desk to hand over the completed case diaries for the SHO to countersign, he was informed that there was a message from the SHO asking him to wait at the police station. The SHO was on his way back from a crime scene and although it would take him about an hour to reach, he wanted Pushpkumar to wait for him. Pushpkumar's hopes of driving down to the river now began fading, and with every passing minute, they became paler still. When the SHO finally reached the police station, it was already late afternoon.

'Jai Hind, sir!' Pushpkumar saluted his senior. 'Santhosh told me that you wanted me to wait for you?' he asked Nair.

'Jai Hind, Pushpkumar,' Nair replied. 'Yes, I want you to visit the scene of occurrence in the Uthra case. It appears that she died due to a snakebite, but her brother suspects some foul play by her husband. The details are in the report recorded by GSI Joy. Ensure that you make a thorough inspection and prepare a detailed *mahazar* (crime scene map).'

'All right, sir. But it is getting dark already. It will be better if I go there tomorrow, sir.'

'Okay. I see your point. But do not delay the visit beyond tomorrow morning, lest the evidence gets disturbed. The scene of occurrence is not more than half-an-hour away and it will be ideal for you to leave early,' Nair ordered. Then, after a moment's thought, he added, 'Tell the residents to not touch anything in the house. We will be treating it as sensitively as a scene of crime. We do not want any alteration of the scene or any accidental tampering of vital clues.'

8 May 2020

'He is a stickler for rules, this Nair. But I do not blame him for it. He has been given a tough assignment. In fact, I am glad he is meticulous in his approach,' Pushpkumar said as he drove his motorcycle to the location of the incident, accompanied by Constable Arun George.

Arun, who was known to not mince his words, responded, 'Sir, you must acknowledge that some of our colleagues have dragged out investigations longer than necessary. They are always struggling to meet deadlines. Inspector Nair has handled them well. And with others like you, in whom he has faith, he hands over challenging cases to them.'

'You are right, Arun. I think Nair smells a rat in this Uthra matter.'

'Yes, sir. There's probably something fishy in the whole case. But let us approach the scene with an open mind. We must hurry up,' Arun sounded determined to charge forward into what promised to be a day of hard-core sleuthing with great focus.

After a few inquiries, Pushpkumar and Arun eventually reached Vishu House, Uthra's parents' residence. The two-storey house was set amid scenic verdant surroundings but was itself in a slightly dilapidated state.

'This house seems to have seen good days. At least that's the impression I gather from looking at it,' Pushpkumar said to Arun and added, 'See if there is someone inside who can open the door.'

Arun replied, 'I can see an old man inside. I am sure he

will let us in. I will also get two neighbours to come with us as witnesses when we prepare the mahazar.'

Arun went and knocked on the door and once the purpose of their visit was described, the police officers were allowed in. They were promptly offered a cup of coffee, but the two policemen refused the offer and got down to work. Arun went out and gathered two of Uthra's parents' neighbours to act as witnesses for the required formalities.

Once everyone was seated, Pushpkumar asked those present, 'Does anyone here know where in the house did the snakebite occur?' He looked at each person, but it seemed that although everyone knew that Uthra had been bitten by a snake, and that she had died as a consequence of it, none of them were in the mood to talk about it too much.

Pushpkumar now began the usual routine of preparing the mahazar, which is drawn roughly to scale. It is an important piece of document that is presented in a court of law when criminal cases are being heard. It helps the judge understand the dimensions of the place, the direction of access and the spaces available for movement, the placement of objects as well as the likely location of the victim(s) and the aggressor(s).

In Uthra's case, the first floor of the house was unconnected to the actual event. The snake had bitten Uthra in the ground floor bedroom where she used to sleep with Sooraj and their son.

Pushpkumar said, 'We will need to make a map of the whole place, beginning with the ground floor. Have you brought the measuring tape, Arun?'

'Yes sir, I have.'

'Let's get going then.'

The whole compound was mapped. The location of the trees, the gate, the water faucets, the shed for the cars, and the driveway, everything was shown on the map. The staircase leading to the first floor was also meticulously measured and recorded. While all the elements and features of the ground and first floor were properly marked, even greater attention was paid to the room where the snakebite had occurred.

'Listen, everyone! Do not touch or move anything. This scene must be preserved exactly as it is now. So be careful about this. Arun and the two witnesses may come in, but please, be very watchful. I repeat, do not touch or move anything in this room,' Pushpkumar announced as soon as they reached the door leading to Uthra's bedroom.

The room was situated in the north-east side of the house and it was sparsely furnished with just two cots, one on the eastern side and the other on the western side.

'The couple appear to have slept on separate beds. That's quite understandable because they have a small child who must have slept with Uthra,' Pushpkumar thought out aloud.

In the mahazar that he was making, he clearly marked the two windows located in the east. There had evidently been an air conditioner in the room at some time, but the holes in the wall meant for its installation were found to be sealed. There was a dressing room to the north side and a bathroom to the west. The dimensions and positions of all the doors, three in total, were recorded on the mahazar.

Pushpkumar then asked Arun to check the underside of the cots for anything out of the ordinary. A thorough inspection of the adjoining dressing room and the bathroom was also carried out.

Pushpkumar and Arun walked over to the windows and looked out at the scene beyond. After a while, Arun turned to Pushpkumar and said, 'These windows are most likely to have been the snake's entry point. We must record their dimensions and their exact height from the ground level.'

'The fact is, Arun, that a snake did enter the room and bite Uthra, and that its venom turned out to be fatal for her. How it found access to the room will only become known to us if we make more inquiries,' Pushpkumar replied. Having finished preparing the mahazar, he added, 'My impression is that this is a simple case of a woman dying because of a snakebite and I sense no foul play. From the few things that we can see lying around in the room, I can tell that they are inconsequential. Let us not take any of these things into our possession as case properties at this stage.'

'As you say, sir. We can tell the people here not to disturb anything and to wait for our clearance before cleaning the room or even touching the objects kept inside it,' said the constable in response.

'Let us put the cordon tape on the entry points to prevent any disturbance of this area,' Pushpkumar advised Arun. 'Inspector Nair told me to be thorough in my preparation of the map. It appears that he is taking the investigation of this incident with a great degree of seriousness.'

On their return to the police station, Pushpkumar briefed SHO Nair about what he had observed. 'Sir, it appears to be an open-and-shut matter. I took the task of preparing the mahazar as seriously as if we were inspecting a scene of murder. But it seems to me that it's simply a snakebite that killed the woman.'

'You know, Uthra's family is not going to be satisfied with that even if you and I are. Haven't we seen enough serious crimes in our careers? In fact, I have the uncanny ability of being able to sniff out a crime from miles afar,' Nair boasted.

9 May 2020

Sooraj's mind was ticking even after the bomb had gone off. He felt a sense of power which is commonly associated with cold-blooded killers—a feeling that is similar to the adrenaline rush that a scalpel-yielding surgeon feels while cutting through a sternum. For a brief moment, you are in a position of absolute power, a position that allows you to take a life, and if the brain goes awry, a Sooraj rises!

Even within the confines of the interrogation room, Sooraj wore a look of achievement. He was too invested in basking in the afterglow of Uthra's demise to observe his grave surroundings. He displayed a haughty, couldn't-care-less demeanour in conditions where even hardened criminals cannot overcome a state of foreboding.

Pushpkumar entered the interrogation room with an expression that gave little away. He was known to employ benign methods of interrogation. He felt that he had been entrusted with the rather difficult task of drawing the final conclusion about the case in just one meeting with Sooraj. When he sat down across the table from Sooraj, he did not waste any time to ask the opening question, 'Sooraj, tell me about the circumstances that led to your wife's death. How was Uthra bitten by the snake?'

Instead of answering the question, Sooraj now started to sob and took some time to collect himself before he replied, 'Sir, you must understand the pain that I am experiencing. I have lost my life partner. What could be a greater tragedy than this?'

'I know it must be tough for you, Sooraj. But you need to tell me about the circumstances which led to this.'

'Sir, I must say that Uthra was an innocent person. She was too trusting, too naive, and despite my pointing out the possibility of danger, she did not take enough precautions. I should tell you that this was not the first time she had been bitten by a dangerous snake.'

Pushpkumar had read in the FIR about the earlier incident with the Russell's viper. Yet, he now pretended as if he was hearing of it for the first time. 'Really? When did that happen?' he asked.

'This was in March, sir. She was bitten on her leg by a Russell's viper, and she had to be hospitalised for over seven weeks. I cared for her during that entire time, and I spent a lot of money to get her the best available treatment because I loved her so much. It was all due to the great love and attention which I gave her that she survived that serious threat to her life.' Sooraj looked up towards the ceiling in a gesture of fake gratitude to God as he said all this.

'Is it not unusual that the same person gets bitten twice by snakes in such quick succession? All of this happened within just two months, right?'

'Yes, it did. And I agree that it must appear unusual. However, I am convinced that there was a curse on Uthra that her end would be caused by snake venom. An astrologer once told me that some people are born with such a curse.'

'Do you believe in that?'

'Yes, sir. Now that it has happened to the love of my life, I have no choice but to say that the astrologer was right.'

'Have you seen any dangerous snakes around the location?'

'Yes sir, I have, and that is why I had warned Uthra to be careful. But she seems to have taken my advice lightly.' After a moment's silence, Sooraj added, 'How I wish now that she had not been taken away from my house to her parents' house after the first incident! Maybe she would have been alive today!'

Pushpkumar understood that the interrogation was leading to only one conclusion: the snakebite was accidental. But he realised that he needed to be sure about this before he could share his conclusions with Nair, so he said to Sooraj, 'What is your mobile number?'

Sooraj blurted out his telephone number with absolute nonchalance. As the SI noted it down, there was a slight smile tugging at the corners of Sooraj's lips. He had already foreseen this move and had deleted his call logs in advance.

When Sooraj left the police station a little while later, he walked out with the swagger of one who had won a battle, and he could barely conceal his glee.

10 May 2020

Pushpkumar was no babe in the woods. The veneer of fortitude that Sooraj had built around himself was not impregnable and the seasoned cop was beginning to see the chinks in it. He had not completely thrown out the possibility of foul play and was therefore not willing to jump to any conclusions based solely on what he had unearthed during Sooraj's brief interrogation.

He made a call to the cyber cell to pass on Sooraj's number for drawing out the latter's call records. He also called A. Prasanthan, a snake rescuer, to understand how snakes behaved. Prasanthan was an unassuming middle-aged man who belonged to the village of Arakkal. He had more than a decade's worth of experience in rescuing snakes and was known to possess deep knowledge about their psychology and behaviour under different circumstances.

Pushpkumar asked, 'Prasanthan, how many times have you heard of people dying of the so-called sarpa dosha? Is it a real phenomenon?'

Prasanthan replied with great confidence, 'Sir, this is absolute nonsense. It is completely unscientific. I do not have any respect for people who explain things like snakebites by bringing in supernatural elements.'

'But Prasanthan, I am aware of a case where one woman was bitten first by a Russell's viper and then just a few weeks later by another dangerous snake. She succumbed to the second bite. Doesn't this prove that she was cursed?'

'No sir, not at all. On the contrary, it proves that there is nothing like a sarpa dosha. Because had she been really cursed, she would have died the first time itself.'

'But she survived because of the medical care she received...'

'Medical care or no medical care, if there actually was a curse, she could not have been saved. If someone is claiming that she was bitten twice because there was a curse on her, let me ask him a few questions. I will prove that he is misinformed. Whoever has told him or her about the existence of a sarpa dosha is actually looking for an opportunity to exploit an inherent fear that most people have of snakes. In such circumstances, people go to great lengths to secure themselves and are willing to spend large sums of money to do so.'

'In the case of this woman, she was bitten on the second occasion in her room on the ground floor of her parents' house. She was living there with her parents, husband, son, and brother. But it beats me how any one of them could have pulled off such a dirty trick!' Pushpkumar said. 'Anyway, Prasanthan, you can leave now.' As the snake rescuer got up and turned to leave, he added, 'Thank you!'

16 May 2020

Pushpkumar and Arun George were on their way to Sooraj's house when Pushpkumar said to his companion, 'Arun, this case is taking a lot of time. When we went to prepare the mahazar the first time, we thought that it was just a routine snakebite case and we would see the end of our probe in one or two days.

Now, even ten days after the occurrence, the story does not seem to be so straightforward.'

'Yes, sir. You are no stranger to the twists and turns that can complicate the tale as an investigation progresses. In this case too, we are not being able to draw a conclusion. The final outcome of our investigation is eluding us. It appeared to be a simple snakebite to begin with, but not anymore,' Arun responded.

'You know, I have learned that Uthra's parents met the SP a couple of days back. They were instigated into doing so because of a bogus complaint of harassment that Sooraj's sister filed against them. Now they are certain that their son-in-law has a hand in their daughter's death.'

'Really? That will make this an even more difficult investigation.'

'Yes. Let us see what decision is taken by the SP.'

As they drove on, Pushpkumar asked Arun, 'Are you superstitious, Arun? Do you believe in something like a sarpa dosha?'

'Sir, back in my village, there is a person who is called by every household when a child is born. He is asked to do some rituals because the people believe that he has the power to protect the newborn from any harm that can be caused by a snake. I have never been convinced that he actually has any of the powers he claims to have. Yet, I do not speak out against him because I do not want to offend him or hurt the feelings of those who believe in him.'

'Haha...Arun! By doing that you allow such balderdash to rule the minds of people.'

Soon enough, the conversation between the two men came to a stop as they turned into the modest house where Sooraj lived; a house which had a name inspired by his: Sree Surya.

'We have our task cut out for us, Arun. We have to collect whatever exhibits we think might have a connection with Uthra's death. I hope you are aware that in March, Uthra was bitten by a Russell's viper here in this house. That is one aspect that we need to keep in our minds as we inspect the premises.'

'Okay, sir.'

At the end of their visit to Sree Surya, among all the things that Pushpkumar and Arun collected and listed in the recovery memo was a bag containing a strip of Estrona Forte Bolus tablets.[15]

GSI Joy, in the meantime, collected the details of Uthra's treatment from the Pushpagiri Medical College Hospital under instructions from Pushpkumar.

On 22 May, the superintendent of police transferred the investigation of the Uthra case to the district-level Crime Branch (CB). The CB was headed by DySP Ashokan. Ashokan was known for his thorough investigations and his ability to extract even the minutest of details through skilful interrogation. He had a team of handpicked investigators to assist him, and he

---

[15] Estrona Forte Bolus + Minarex Bolus is a unique combination of *bhasmas* which has important minerals and medicinal herbs that encourage the growth of underdeveloped genital organs, stimulate ovulatory heat, and also regulate the oestrus cycle in dairy animals.

used the method of brainstorming to prepare a list of probable perpetrators and accomplices. Ashokan's investigation of Uthra's death began on 23 May.

23 May 2020

Ashokan was closeted with his team and he started the brainstorming session with a question that was playing on everyone's mind: 'Do you think this is a murder case or just a normal death caused by a snakebite?'

There was silence in the room. After a while, Ashokan asked the same question again. This time, GSI Rameshkumar, known for making fast conclusions, said, 'Sir, snakebites are common in this area. Why should we doubt anybody?'

'What do you say, Anilkumar?' Ashokan asked.

GSI Anilkumar, gifted with a sharp analytical brain and the ability to always look at issues from different angles, responded, 'Sir, in my opinion, we need to look at the possible motives that anyone might have had to kill Uthra. Who were the people who are likely to have gained anything from her death? What could have been the stakes involved? What could be gained from killing the mother of an infant, and that too a woman who was differently abled and whose mental prowess was quite low? Moreover, we have never heard of snakes being used as a weapon of murder.'

Ashokan then informed everyone present that the constable who was on duty at the district morgue had called a little while back and told him that an examination of the deceased's viscera had revealed the presence of snake poison and that on this basis, the cause of death was identified as envenomation.

Anilkumar spoke again, 'Clearly, there is no doubt that the cause of death is indeed the presence of snake poison. We now have to examine how this venom entered Uthra's body to cause her death, and whether it was some human being who was responsible for it.'

Grade Assistant Sub Inspector (GASI) Manojkumar, who was often the last to react in such discussions, suddenly got animated, 'Sir, to my mind, only one man could have gained anything from killing Uthra, and that's her husband. We need to examine Sooraj's relationship with her from every angle. We have to see what role he might have played in bringing a snake into the picture. What prompted him to take such a ghastly step?' After a moment's thought, he resumed, 'But the death was caused by snakebite. How could he cause this to happen? And using a snake to kill someone, that is unheard of….'

Ashokan shook his head and said, 'No, using snakes for committing a murder is not an entirely unknown phenomenon. I have heard of snakebite murders having taken place in some other states. I can't recall the specific cases, but I know for sure that this is not the first time in our country that something like this has happened, although it is true that Kerala has not seen such a case before. Uthra's parents have come up with the allegation that their son-in-law is responsible for the death of their daughter. Their suspicion cannot be brushed aside lightly. We'll have to probe deep to figure this case out.'

For once it was Manojkumar who reacted immediately, 'Sir, on the one hand we are all in agreement that it is a snakebite that is the cause of death, and on the other, we are not dismissing the suspicion raised by Vijayasenan and Manimekhala. How can this be explained?'

Anilkumar offered his thoughts, 'Strange things happen all the time, Manojkumar. Let us not dismiss any theory right now, no matter how incredible it might appear. As it is, we have just taken up the case and as we proceed with the probe, we will encounter different possibilities—'

Ashokan interrupted Anilkumar, 'Let us not forget that in March also Uthra was bitten by a Russell's viper. That's just two months back. Does it not raise questions about how she survived one snakebite only to become a victim of another? I see in this a very good reason to suspect foul play.'

After a while, Ashokan got up from his chair and started to pace the room. His movements were that of a man who was in deep contemplation. Every time he turned, he looked at the group assembled in the room. They were all sleuths with years of experience and high levels of skill in their profession. It seemed as if he was mentally going over the comments that had been made a little while earlier by each of them.

'All of you have made valid points,' Ashokan said as he sat back in his chair. He looked right into the eyes of Rameshkumar and continued, 'Yes, an understanding of the motive will throw light on many things, including likely suspects.' He then looked at Anilkumar and said, 'As for the method of introducing the fatal dose of snake venom into the victim's bloodstream, that will have to be worked out with the help of toxinologists.[16] Herpetologists will also be helpful, just as snake wranglers and

[16] Experts in the study of venoms.

medical doctors would be.' Ashokan remained silent for a couple of minutes while he tried to sum up his thoughts. He then turned to GASI Manojkumar and said, 'I agree that Sooraj seems to have the most tangible reason to go for something as extreme a step as murder. We can keep him as our primary suspect, but let us not confine all our thoughts to just one suspect. All of you, please keep your thinking caps on and don't be limited by any of the seemingly obvious facts.'

Ashokan now took out a file from a drawer in his table and with great flair, he pulled out an envelope from within the file. 'This has come from the cyber cell,' he announced, his eagerness to immediately dive into its contents palpable. He opened the envelope and quickly pulled out the sheaf of papers inside. They were all neatly printed statements from a mobile phone service provider.

'These are Sooraj's call records. Let us have a close look at these.'

The attention of all those sitting around the table was fixed on the papers in Ashokan's hands and everyone looked at them expectantly.

'The examination of the call records needs to be a systematic exercise, as all of you already know. Let us pay close attention and keep a lookout for any number which Sooraj might have called repeatedly or from which he might have received several calls. I am dividing the pages equally. We will highlight any numbers which appear repeatedly in the pages we get.'

The entire team was immersed in studying the papers for a couple of hours. At the end of this process, they matched the numbers highlighted by each one of them and found that a large number of calls had been made to one particular number. Luckily, they were also able to find this number in their station's records. It belonged to a snake wrangler named Chavarukavu Suresh. Ashokan said he knew of a snake wrangler by that name who had gained fame by putting out videos of snake rescues on a YouTube channel. When they looked for Chavarukavu Suresh's YouTube channel, they found that the profile image on the channel showed a man with a snake in his hand, which added credence to what Ashokan had said.

'Sir, it appears quite likely that this snake wrangler has played a role in the entire affair. He has clearly been in touch with Sooraj lately. This lead should take us somewhere, don't you think?' saying so, Manojkumar examined Ashokan's expression to see if there was a look of approval on his senior's face.

Ashokan agreed, 'Of course, Manojkumar. One can conclude that the needle of suspicion is now pointing at both Sooraj and Suresh. I think we have come to a point where we can interrogate these two. Hopefully, that will help us acquire greater clarity.' After a pause, he added, 'Let us go get them!'

INTERROGATION

23 May 2020

Ashokan exchanged notes with SI Pushpkumar before interrogating Sooraj. He was not surprised to learn about the confidence that Sooraj had exuded in his interaction with Pushpkumar. With so many years of experience under his belt, Ashokan knew that some minds were free of guilt and full of self-admiration even when caught within the adverse confines of a police station's interrogation room. He also had a word with SP Hari Sankar to understand some of the technical terms that he had come across while going through the available intel. Ashokan then devised a strategy to break through Sooraj's bravado and summoned him to the police station.

The first part of Ashokan's strategy was to make Sooraj wait. It was afternoon when the latter walked into the police station. The weather was extremely sultry and Ashokan wanted his suspect to literally feel the heat. So he instructed a home guard on duty to cut off the power supply to the fan in the interrogation room and let Sooraj stew in the heat and humidity for quite a while.

There was an irate look on Sooraj's face when Ashokan finally walked into the interrogation room after about an hour. He glared at Ashokan almost as if he were the suspect.

'I hear your chat with Pushpkumar went well. He tells me there is little reason to suspect you,' Ashokan lied.

'It was okay. Please turn on the fan.' Sooraj wiped the beads of sweat off his forehead.

'The fan is not working. Fortunately, those of us who are from the Crime Branch are used to hot pursuits!' Ashokan said in a sarcastic tone.

'Is this how you treat an innocent man?' Sooraj demanded and threw his hands up in exasperation.

'Used to comfort, aren't you?'

'What do you mean?'

'Nothing. I could not help but notice from the case diaries that your standard of living has improved considerably after your marriage.'

Sooraj's face registered the slightest degree of fear for the first time.

Ashokan continued, 'So, how much money did you get as dowry?'

'Sir! There was no such demand that we made,' Sooraj said emphatically.

'Really? Strange. I have been told that your wife's, sorry, your late wife's parents think otherwise.'

'Sir, to be very honest, they never really liked me. So I am not surprised that they are spewing all kinds of nonsensical things about me.'

'Be a little considerate Sooraj. They have just lost a very capable daughter.'

'Capable?' Sooraj scoffed.

'Have I said something that you don't agree with?'

Sooraj kept silent for a bit and then mumbled something to himself.

'It seems to me that there is a lot you are holding within yourself, Sooraj. How about we take a break?' Ashokan asked. But before Sooraj could answer, he had already walked out of the room.

This little interaction had made Sooraj very nervous. He could sense that Ashokan was onto something and he desperately wanted to outwit him. He started thinking of all the things he would have to steer clear of in a full-fledged round of questioning. Suresh was on the top of that list.

Ashokan returned half an hour later with a bundle of papers which he kept on the lone table in the room. Sooraj was bathed in sweat by now. Ashokan passed him a towel, but he promptly refused it.

'So where were we?' Ashokan asked. 'Don't like your in-laws much, huh?'

'Nothing like that, sir. On the contrary, I have always been nice to them.'

'I am sure that is the case. In fact, it's clearly reflected in Vijayasenan's bank statement too!'

'Sir, I was going to return that money.'

'So it was never a demand for dowry?'

'No, sir. I borrowed the money only because I wanted to take care of my wife and child.'

Ashokan moved towards the table in the room and began looking through the papers he had kept there. Unknown to Sooraj, most of these were blank sheets of paper meant just as dramatic props to heighten the psychological impact of the interrogation on Sooraj. As he watched Ashokan flip through nearly a hundred sheets of paper one at a time, the wait for the genie that he knew the policeman was going to pull out had his heart thumping loudly.

Eventually, Ashokan pulled out a sheet of paper from the middle of the pile and thrust it into Sooraj's face. 'I am sure the person on the other side of this number was also helping you take proper care of your family?' he said sarcastically.

'Sir, I did not understand,' Sooraj mumbled. He gulped down some saliva as he saw his call records printed on the paper in front of him, with Suresh's number clearly highlighted. He had not known that just deleting his call history would not have taken care of the data that had already been recorded on the server of his network service provider.

'Really? I thought you know a lot about snakes and curses. You almost turned my colleague Pushpkumar into a believer of the supernatural.'

Sooraj kept mum.

'The person to whom this number belongs is also being interrogated as we speak. Luckily for us, he is singing like a bird,' Ashokan lied again. The truth was that Suresh had not yet been called for questioning, but Ashokan wanted to rattle Sooraj and get more leads before they conducted Suresh's interrogation.

'Sir, do not believe him. He has an agenda.'

'I see. Does everyone have an agenda to frame you, Sooraj?'

'Sir, I am innocent. You need to believe me.'

'Hold that thought and that look of innocence while we take another break.'

This interruption was soothing for Sooraj, but it also led to a great deal of confusion in his mind. He knew that he would have to change his version of events since his connection to Suresh had already been found out. He realised that the only way to save his skin now would be to place the entire blame at Suresh's doorstep.

This break in Sooraj's interrogation was shorter than the previous one. Ashokan did not want to give him enough time to refine and rework the latest version of his story.

'Shall we resume?' Ashokan asked as he walked into the room.

Sooraj nodded.

'How do you know Suresh?'

'Sir, he is a snake wrangler. I used to watch his videos on YouTube.'

'I see. When and where did this interest that you have in snakes take root?'

'Sir, a lot of snakes had been spotted in our locality and I was looking for someone who could conduct a workshop to sensitise people to snakes.'

'And you found your mentor in Suresh?' Ashokan looked Sooraj in the eye.

'Yes, sir. He has a lot of skill in capturing and rescuing snakes. I knew that the people in my locality needed an awareness drive about snakes.'

'Go on.'

'So I got in touch with him and he agreed to visit the village.'

'And you made all these phone calls to Suresh just to convince him about this workshop?'

'No, sir. He actually became greedy and started demanding money.'

'The case file clearly indicates just how likely you are to have parted with your money. Did you agree to pay him?'

There was no right answer here. Sooraj looked away from Ashokan and began to anticipate what Suresh might say during his interrogation.

'Welcome back!' Ashokan said when Sooraj finally resumed eye contact with him.

'Yes, I agreed to pay him. After all, it was meant for the good of the people,' he said in a feeble tone.

'So large-hearted of you, Sooraj. But do you take me to be a fool?' Ashokan said aggressively.

'Sir, believe me, please,' Sooraj pleaded.

'Okay. I will hear you out. Go on then!'

'Sir, when Suresh came for the demonstration, he was very careless,' Sooraj began constructing a likely series of events. 'He did not keep the snake secure and ultimately, he lost sight of it while attempting to show off his skills after the workshop.'

'Which snake was this?'

'Sir, it was a Russell's viper.'

'Was it not a cobra that delivered the fatal bite?'

'That was the second time Uthra was bit, sir.'

'Oh right! There are two instances of snakebite that we are considering. Quite a coincidence, don't you think?'

Seeing himself cornered, Sooraj turned to the supernatural once again, 'Sir, it has to be the serpent's curse!'

Ashokan got up from his seat and dragged the table in the room close to Sooraj. He now sat on it and gave him a rather matter-of-fact glance as he said, 'Suresh is in my custody too. And like I told you already, he is talking. It will be best if you cut the bullshit and stick to the truth. I am throwing you into the lockup for the night. It will do you good if your thoughts are clearer by the time day breaks and we resume this interrogation.'

Even as Sooraj begged Ashokan to let him go and made repeated assertions about his innocence, Ashokan paid him no heed and simply left the room. Suresh was not yet in the custody of the police. However, Sooraj had now given Ashokan enough cause to make him summon Suresh as a suspect. He instructed a constable to get Suresh to the police station in the morning. In the meantime, Ashokan wanted to go through the case diaries and Pushpkumar's neatly made mahazar again because these were of great value in framing the right questions.

24 May 2020

Ashokan had not slept well. He had tossed and turned through most of the night in anticipation of the interrogations that were

Visual of a bite made naturally.

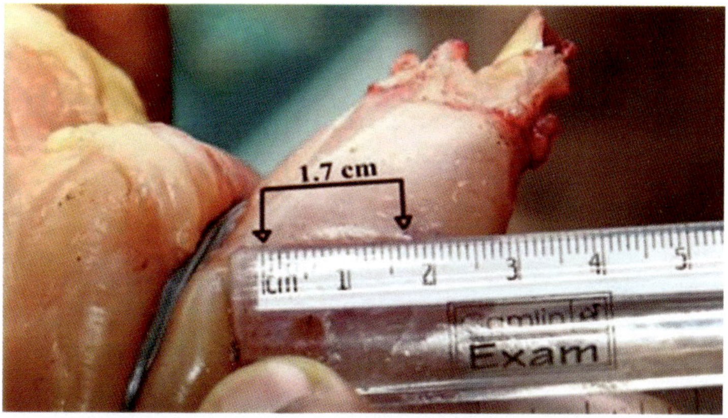

Measurement of a natural bite.

The bedroom where the incident took place.

scheduled for the following day. A feminist at heart, Ashokan wanted Uthra to get justice. All that mattered to him was to get to the bottom of the case. Even if it was a simple case of snakebite, he needed to know the truth. His curiosity had effectively robbed him of precious hours of sleep.

Ashokan revisited the case diaries early in the morning. He then went out for a stroll near his house and while out walking, he decided upon a line of questioning. He also thought of a plan B in case things took a sudden and unwanted turn.

As Ashokan entered the police station later that morning, he was told that Suresh was already there. He asked for him to be sent to the interrogation room and told a home guard to fix and restore the power connection to the fan.

'Suresh...the YouTube sensation himself!' Ashokan announced as he entered the interrogation room.

Suresh stood up to greet Ashokan. He was used to being in the company of cops and wanted to make a good first impression.

'Sit down, sit down, Suresh. I hear that you have been a valuable resource person for the police till now,' Ashokan said.

'I am always at your service, sir,' Suresh replied humbly.

'And how about Sooraj? Were you on his payroll too?' Ashokan suddenly deflected the conversation into choppy waters.

'Sir, I don't know what you are talking about.'

'Really? That's interesting, because Sooraj has been talking about you like you are his mentor. He seems to be convinced that all he knows about snakes is thanks to your teaching.'

'Sir, he got in touch with me to learn about snakes.'

'The staff at the police station tells me that you are not exactly a social person. Then why this soft corner for Sooraj?'

'Sir, I am always willing to help those who wish to learn about reptiles.'

'So you have a grain of charity in you, is it? You like to do social service?'

'Yes, sir.'

'Then why did you take money from Sooraj for the demonstration?' Ashokan played his trump card.

Suresh knew that the interrogation was going to be a rough ride. He feared that Uthra's death was directly related to the snakes he had supplied to Sooraj. But he did not want to face any punishment and decided to act innocent.

'Sir, I am not aware of any such exchange,' Suresh mumbled.

'I am sure you are not. That is why you took so long to answer. So Sooraj is lying about the money then?'

'Sir, I think he has mistaken me for someone else.' Even as he said this, Suresh found it hard to make sense of his own statement.

'You have a twin brother?' Ashokan laughed.

'Haha!' Suresh allowed a smile to slip through.

'So Sooraj gave Rs 8,000 to an impostor it seems....' Ashokan shook his head.

'I don't know anything about the money, sir.'

'But you did conduct the workshop?'

'Yes, sir. But I never got Rs 10,000!'

'I said eight. Not ten.' Ashokan looked at Suresh intently.

'Umm....Sorry, sir. I meant eight.' Suresh flushed guiltily.

'Suresh, I know you are not a cold-blooded criminal. Come on now, speak the truth.'

This was met with no response from the snake wrangler. Suresh suddenly started to feel a tingling sensation in his deformed middle finger and he began fidgeting a little. Ashokan's keen eyes immediately noticed this shift in his body language.

'I know you have sacrificed a lot, Suresh,' Ashokan said placatingly. 'I am on your side, believe me. Please tell me the truth.' Playing the good cop came quite naturally to the ace detective.

Suresh began to sob.

'Suresh, tell me the truth!' Ashokan persisted.

'Sir, it was all him. I have done nothing wrong.'

'Who?'

Suresh retreated into a stoic silence. He had run out of 'right' answers.

'I will get your partner-in-crime here and then we will see what you both have to say.'

'Sooraj is here?' Suresh felt the ground literally slip away from under his feet.

'Yes, he is. I am glad you have not forgotten his name,' Ashokan mocked.

'Sir, I just supplied the snakes. I did not know that he was hatching this diabolical plot,' Suresh said in a resigned tone.

'We will see about that!' Ashokan retorted, sounding triumphant. He stepped out of the interrogation room and turned up the fan speed as he did. Suresh looked at the fan while it drowned out the sound of his sobbing.

Ashokan had stuck to the line of questioning he had visualised during his morning walk, and clearly, it had worked. However, he was also keen on putting plan B into action now—interrogating Sooraj and Suresh together.

Mentor and mentee were huddled together in the interrogation room. This was their first meeting after the death of Uthra. The bluntest knife could have cut through the unease that hung heavy in the air inside the room. Not a word was spoken by either suspect. They made eye contact with each other a couple of times, but then immediately looked away. Sooraj noticed that the fan in the interrogation room had been repaired.

Ashokan was sipping on his coffee and conversing with the SHO who had fixed himself a masala tea.

'The thorough work done by your team has been of great help. Rarely does the CB come across cases where the local police have been so diligent,' Ashokan complimented the chief of the police station.

'Thank you, sir. I am actually very concerned about the upward trend in the crime graph. The only way to deal with this situation is to be thorough in all our work.' Nair wore a look of great pride as he said this.

'What do you make of this case, Nair? I know we are handling it now, but any inputs from you and your team would be useful and very welcome,' Ashokan said.

'Sir, it is very kind of you to have asked for my opinion. At first, I felt that this was a simple case of a woman dying of a snakebite, but my impression has changed considerably since then. I think we must give the first instance of snakebite as much importance as the second one. If the killer's intent was strong enough to push him or her to make a second attempt even after seeing Uthra's pain during her treatment at the Pushpagiri Hospital, we are dealing with a heartless murderer. I think this crime carries the weight of not one but two murders.' Nair's tenor was laden with heartbreak. He had evidently been moved by the victim's plight.

'Nair, I am often told that empathising with the victim is not the job of a cop. But in your rather emotional statement, I have found multiple angles that only a gifted sleuth can explore. I am sure these angles will help me in the interrogation. Now let me show our suspects exactly what they are up against.'

Ashokan got up from his chair and quickly walked towards the interrogation room. Nair stood up as his senior left.

Half an hour had passed since Sooraj and Suresh had been sitting inside the interrogation room with their shoulders slumped and their heads hanging low. They were both sweating profusely in spite of the fan being at full speed.

Ashokan entered the room a little while later with a swagger in his stride. He straightened his collar, made eye contact with both the shifty suspects, and placed a heap of papers on the table in the room.

'So, how are the brothers in arms doing?'

Sooraj and Suresh stole a quick look at each other after hearing Ashokan's tenor.

'There is no point in crying over spilt milk. It is time to talk!' Ashokan then looked at Suresh and said, 'Let's begin with you.'

Suresh's chair creaked as he shifted in his seat. He felt weak in his knees and was incessantly rubbing his deformed finger.

'Sooraj tells me you killed Uthra!' Ashokan announced.

'No! No! Sir, I had nothing to do with the murder. I swear on my daughter. I just supplied the snake.' Suresh sounded desperate.

'Liar! It is because of *your* carelessness that my wife is dead!' Sooraj exclaimed.

'Ahan! You two are finally on talking terms, is it?' Ashokan chuckled.

Suresh slipped from his chair and all but sank to the ground as he held on to Ashokan's left leg. He started wailing loudly. These antics were enough to make Sooraj conscious of the need for some drama of his own. He copied Suresh's actions and caught hold of Ashokan's right leg. The chorus of the wailing was as discordant as the crime being dealt with.

'Shut up! I have no mercy for criminals!' Ashokan stood up hastily and took a step back to free himself of the two men. 'I have enough evidence to arrest you both. If there is something you wish to say, now is the time.'

'Sir, I am sorry. I should not have supplied the snake to this man, but sir, I really had nothing to do with the murder,' Suresh pleaded.

By now, Sooraj had retreated into a strange silence, and even a seasoned interrogator like Ashokan was unable to understand this sudden shift in the man's body language.

'The cat is out of the bag, Sooraj. Or should I say the snake is out of the jar?'

Sooraj stared at Ashokan with a menacing look on his face.

'I have it on good authority that you treated Uthra with disdain. Just imagine her plight. She had to care for her child, face her own disability, and then, on top of everything, also deal with an abusive husband. You have sullied the name of our great state!'

The menace on Sooraj's face grew.

'You tortured an innocent woman. Did you kill her? Tell me you, bastard!' The use of expletives did not come naturally to Ashokan, but he meant this one.

'Shut up!' Sooraj exclaimed. This was as good as a confession for Ashokan. He knew Sooraj was now close to breaking point.

'At least Suresh has done some good for society. He is not a dishonourable man like you!' Ashokan continued, deliberately trying to needle Sooraj.

This comparison was too much for Sooraj to digest.

'I am going to kill you too!' he shouted. 'You are nothing but a filthy cop. You don't know who I am, *maire*.'[17]

'No, you won't kill me. You only prey on the helpless and the weak.'

'You would have understood my situation had your wife been mentally challenged.'

Ashokan kept quiet. He knew Sooraj would talk more.

'You idiots think that everyone can be lectured on the rights of women. But I am not weak like you. I got rid of my problem once and for all, and I have no regrets now. None whatsoever!'

Ashokan moved around the room and waited for his own anger to settle. He had managed to draw out a confession from

---

[17] A Malayali expletive.

Sooraj and did not want to let his efforts go down the drain with an unwanted emotional overreaction.

'Take these two men away,' he called out to the home guard on duty finally. 'Let's get the paperwork for their arrest ready.'

Suresh had started crying uncontrollably by now, while Sooraj still looked agitated.

Ashokan knew that pinning the crime on the duo would be a tall order. The case was going to be built largely on circumstantial evidence which would have to be gathered quickly. Every passing minute was a minute being taken away from a chance at justice for Uthra. Instead of taking a break after the interrogation, Ashokan headed straight for the SHO's desk. He also asked the rest of his team from the Crime Branch to assemble. There was a lot that needed to be done, and the sooner they got cracking, the better it would be.

SLEUTHING

24 May 2020

It was SP Hari Sankar who had transferred Uthra's case to the Crime Branch on 22 May. With his background in technology (he held a master's degree in Robotics), he understood the various scientific angles which came into play in the investigation. It was clear to him that such an intricate probe could not be effectively carried out by officers from an already overburdened police station. Bringing in the district Crime Branch was a necessary step to ensure that the investigation could be a dedicated process that was not hampered by other day-to-day tasks. He was confident that the Crime Branch was ideally suited to drive the investigation on scientific lines, more so since the case had landed in the able hands of A. Ashokan. Sankar wanted to continue playing a supervisory role in the investigation and he called a meeting to discuss the road forward.

During the meeting, an SIT with Hari Sankar at the helm, Ashokan as his deputy, and other officers from the Crime Branch was constituted to focus on the case. All the available inputs, including the statements recorded till then were discussed.

The importance of an in-depth study of the various electronic devices used by the accused for scouring data was stressed by Hari Sankar. He also defined roles in the team and made it clear that his role was supervisory while Ashokan's involvement in the probe would be of the go-to leader, the investigating officer.

Hari Sankar pointed out that the investigation could very well become one with multiple dimensions, and that the team would need a senior officer to do all the back-room work like maintenance of records. The day-to-day coordination of the work done by different team members operating from various locations would also have to be dovetailed to keep the narrative watertight. S. Madhusoodanan, the additional SP of Kollam rural district, was handed this key responsibility.

Hari Sankar also proposed the last-minute addition of Civil Police Officer Mahesh Mohan to the investigation team. Posted in the Kollam Cyber Cell, Mohan was a Microsoft certified systems engineer. He had secured the first rank in the entrance examination conducted by Kerala Police to select personnel with computer awareness. He had also attended workshops in cyber forensics.

The SIT lost no time in taking decisive steps. They reckoned that there were enough facts to conclude that Uthra's death was no accident. Her parents could not be faulted for suspecting foul play by their son-in-law.

As a follow-up of the SIT's conclusion, Ashokan incorporated the offences under Sections 115 (Abetment of offence punishable with death or imprisonment for life), 326 (Voluntarily causing grievous hurt by dangerous weapons or means), 307 (Attempt to murder), 302 (Murder), and 34 (Acts done by several persons in furtherance of common intention) of the Indian Penal Code (IPC) and forwarded his reports to the court of the sub-divisional magistrate, Punalur, and the concerned judicial magistrate.

After these formalities, he arrested Suresh and Sooraj on 24 May.

A body search of both the suspects was conducted post their arrest and their mobile phones were seized in the presence of cyber-expert Mahesh Mohan.

25 May 2020

Vishu House was now officially a scene of murder. Ashokan's team from the Crime Branch got down to the business of collecting evidence with its usual quiet efficiency. They also got a handcuffed Sooraj along with them to corroborate parts of the statements he had made earlier to Ashokan.

The ground floor bedroom was scanned very carefully. The mahazar prepared by Pushpkumar was now compared with what was actually there at the scene. Assisted by a head constable, GASI Manojkumar, who was an old hand at analysing crime scenes, went inch-by-inch through the entire length and breadth of the room, only to come up with a rather short conclusion, 'Pushpkumar has done a thorough job. Good!'

In the meantime, Ashokan led the highly organised process of collecting objects of evidentiary value. He had knowledge of umpteen cases where seemingly insignificant bits and pieces had filled important blanks in working out crimes under the scanner. While the team was collecting evidence inside the compound, Ashokan sieved through the immediate surroundings with Sooraj in tow.

During his interrogation, Sooraj had mentioned that Suresh had brought the snake responsible for Uthra's death in a plastic jar. Ashokan knew that the jar was a vital piece of material evidence. Its discovery would bring to the police the advantage of Section 27 of the Indian Evidence Act.[18] So he asked Sooraj about the location of the plastic jar as they moved around the locality. A habitual liar, Sooraj started to feign ignorance. By now, however, Ashokan knew the most effective ways to jog his prime suspect's memory.

'Do you want me to help you recall what you are forgetting? You have to give me proof that Suresh has a role to play in your wife's death. And if this is not enough, I have medicines that can help in the case of memory loss. Don't forget that you said it in your statement as well—that you had concealed the plastic jar somewhere around here. Now is the time to prove that you were

---

[18] Statements made to police officers during an investigation are not admissible as evidence under the provisions of Section 25 of the Indian Evidence Act. However, there is a rider to this blanket provision, as described in Section 27 of the same act which states: 'How much of information received from an accused may be proved: Provided that, when any fact is deposed to as discovered in consequence of information received from a person accused of any offence, in the custody of a police officer, so much of such information, whether it amounts to a confession or not, as relates distinctly to the fact thereby discovered, may be proved.' The recovery of the plastic jar would fall under this provision.

not bluffing.' Saying so, Ashokan began transferring the baton he was carrying from one hand to the other. This not-so-subtle signal was enough to suddenly bring back Sooraj's memory.

'Yes, I remember everything now!' he exclaimed. 'I hid it behind an old uninhabited house nearby. Let's go there.'

Sooraj quickly led Ashokan to the house he had just mentioned and pointed to a pile of garbage in its backyard. 'It's there! I am not a liar. You can check for yourself.'

Sure enough, Ashokan's men recovered the plastic jar from the garbage pile. It had been lying concealed under some cadjan[19] and coconut husk. Great care was taken while collecting the jar, and latent fingerprints[20] were lifted by an expert present on the spot. It was necessary for the investigating officer to collect evidence that would corroborate Sooraj's claim that the recovered plastic jar was indeed the one in which Suresh had handed over the cobra to him. For this purpose, it was decided that the DNA of the dead snake, when recovered, would be matched with the DNA found inside the jar.

Apart from the plastic jar, a black shoulder bag, a transparent bottle, a nightgown, a bed sheet, and a skirt were also recovered from Uthra's house among other innocuous looking objects.

---

19 Cadjan are woven mats made from coconut palm leaves. They are generally used for roofing and as walls.

20 Chance impressions, or what are more commonly known as latent fingerprints, are the oftentimes invisible patterns made by fingerprints that are usually left at crime investigations or on objects recovered from crime scenes, and forensically analysed by latent fingerprint experts with the application of chemical or physical methods. ('Latent Fingerprint,' Encyclopedia.com)

That same evening, Renjith Babu, who was working as a Tester Inspector in the Kerala Police District Finger Print Bureau, confirmed that the latent fingerprints which had been lifted from the plastic jar matched the right thumbprint and the right ring fingerprint of Sooraj. This was a major breakthrough for the investigators.

Material evidence is what gives an investigator the ammunition for framing probing questions when interrogating the accused persons and the witnesses. The Crime Branch team had collected enough evidence from the scene of occurrence to smell the smoking gun out, or in this case, the hissing cobra.

Ashokan's team began to analyse the evidentiary value of what had been collected as soon as they got back to the police station. They started with Sooraj's mobile phone which had been seized upon his arrest. It was a key object that could connect him to the people he would have contacted to facilitate Uthra's murder. Mahesh Mohan was in-charge of ensuring that no slips were made in the examination.

Mobile phones are a ubiquitous device these days. While they are used by criminals in the process of committing crimes, they also serve as an excellent piece of electronic evidence which investigators can use for digging out a lot of vital information. Smart phones are even more valuable in this respect. All the information that is exchanged on WhatsApp and other apps either as text or audio messages, the video channels and the photographs that are viewed, the websites that are accessed, the calls that are made, everything is laden with priceless little nuggets which skilful investigators exploit with the help of cyber and IT experts to build up a cohesive picture of both the crime and the criminal(s).

Mohan now dug into Sooraj's search engine history. There were countless searches that had been made regarding *Kuzhimandali* snakes (Russell's viper), other vipers, *Moorkhan* snakes (Indian cobra), and snake wrangler C. Suresh. His YouTube search history was also full of searches related to snakes. In fact, the last search on Google was about the Russell's viper. All this clearly established that the person using that particular mobile device was not only keenly gathering knowledge about venomous snakes, but was also following C. Suresh's every move.

Apart from the recovery of the device itself, it was also extremely important to establish that it belonged to Sooraj, and this had to be done on the basis of the data extracted from the device. Mohan found that the Play Store application on the Android device had been synced with the e-mail ID surajskumar1993@*****.com, which was the email ID that Sooraj used. He also found the screenshot of an email that Sooraj had sent to the office of Kerala's chief minister, and the digital signature attached to the mail was one that had been signed in Sooraj's handwriting; this was later confirmed as being a perfect match by a handwriting expert.

Two mobile phones had also been seized from Suresh. On a close and thorough inspection of the WhatsApp history of one of the mobiles, Mohan found Sooraj's number saved in the device's contact list as 'HDFC Adoor Bank'. Several pictures of snakes had been sent from this device to Sooraj's mobile. Sooraj, on the other hand, had saved Suresh's number as 'Suresh Snake'.

Since the workshop conducted by Suresh had been recorded by his colleague Premjith, his mobile phone was also collected as evidence. In the picture gallery on this device, Mohan located three images of Sooraj and Suresh standing together, and a video of Sooraj handling a snake under the supervision of Suresh.

A missing piece in the trail of evidence was the exchange of the cobra. SP Hari Sankar was of the view that if the cobra had indeed come from Suresh, then he would have had to meet Sooraj to hand it over, and the location where the two men must have met could be determined by tracking the location history of their respective cell phones. Mohan immediately caught on to the idea. The triangulation[21] of data from three mobile towers placed Sooraj and Suresh near a pan shop known as Ajeem Pan Shop, close to the Enathu old market, on 24 April. A detailed sketch of the location was soon prepared. Mohan also prepared route maps for both suspects by coordinating the latitude and longitude of the mobile towers.

---

[21] Triangulation is a technique used to identify the location of mobile devices. The prerequisite is that the device being tracked should be receiving signals from three or more mobile towers. The point of overlap of these signals makes it possible to estimate the location of the device based on its distance from any of the three mobile towers. The mobile towers broadcast their location and by plotting the distance of the device from each tower, its co-ordinates are calculated. In urban areas where there are many mobile towers, triangulation is commonly employed for tracking.

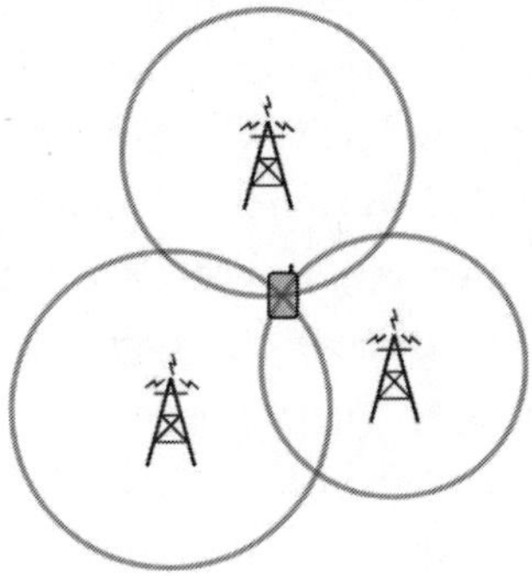

A representative diagram of the process of triangulation

The investigation team found an ATM belonging to the Ezhamkulam South Indian Bank close to this location. The ATM's closed-circuit television (CCTV) footage was retrieved with the help of the bank manager. It had captured Sooraj withdrawing money from the ATM around the time of his meeting with Suresh on 24 April. The transaction was then traced back to Sooraj's ATM card for further corroboration. The CCTV footage also showed him carrying a black shoulder bag, the possession of which he had denied during his interrogation. This discovery indicated a possible exchange of money between Sooraj and Suresh. The SIT concluded that this was directly linked to the handing over of the cobra.

Armed with incriminating pointers which implicated Sooraj in the murder, Ashokan sought to keep him in police custody for further investigation, and was granted this custody till 30

May. It was during this period of internment that Sooraj, when confronted with all the evidence collected thus far, found no way of denying that he knew where the carcass of the snake was buried. He finally had to tell the police just where to look in Uthra's parents' property, and basis the location he gave to the investigators, the decaying carcass was exhumed from a block of soil on 26 May. Its necropsy[22] was conducted on the spot by a veterinary surgeon, Dr Kishore Kumar, and other forensic experts. Samples of the decomposed parts of the snake along with some soil were carefully collected by the team as exhibits and sent to the Rajiv Gandhi Centre for Biotechnology, Thiruvananthapuram.

The DNA extracted from the carcass did not conclusively match the DNA recovered from the plastic jar. It was, however, proved that the jar contained traces of the DNA of the species *Naja Naja* or the Indian Cobra. A biotechnologist at the Rajiv Gandhi Centre for Biotechnology confirmed that the DNA from the scales, muscles, bones, and fangs of the exhumed snake also belonged to the species Indian Cobra.

The SIT finally had a name to put on the murder weapon: Indian Cobra!

The cobra, or any other member of the snake family for that matter, is seen as a danger and a threat by most people. But the cobra itself is listed among the endangered species, and its protection is secured by wildlife law. When the remains of a dead cobra were recovered from the compound of Uthra's house, a case under the Wild Life (Protection) Act was registered by

[22] Necropsy is the post-mortem examination of an animal species.

the forest department against Suresh, the snake wrangler who had caught the serpent, and against Sooraj, who had unlawfully acquired it. This further strengthened the case that the police was building against both the men.

Later at Sree Surya, Ashokan had the mahazar of Uthra's first floor room made. This was the room where in March 2020 she had been bitten by a Russell's viper. The location from where Suresh had caught the viper in question was also mapped by Ashokan's team.

On 29 May, Ashokan went to Vishu House to have a fresh look at the bedroom where Uthra had been bitten fatally. The bedroom was situated in the north-eastern portion of the ground floor. Under Ashokan's directions, all dimensions of the room along with its features, like the number and location of its windows and doors, were meticulously re-recorded. All potential entry points for a snake were also mapped.

During this visit, Ashokan seized the stick that Sooraj and Vijayan Vishu had used to kill the snake. A bedsheet that had been used by Uthra and her mobile phone were also added to the evidence pool. On Uthra's phone, some WhatsApp chats with Sooraj were found which demonstrated her faith in him. Ashokan also got Sooraj's Baleno car, which was standing parked in the premises, examined by a scientific assistant, who recovered a strip of Monty LC[23] tablets from beneath the floor mat of the

[23] A chemical combination of Montelukast and Levocetrizine.

driver's seat. The strip had eight empty pockets and two tablets that were still intact.

On seeing the strip of tablets, Vijayasenan asked Ashokan for a word. 'Sir, on the day of Uthra's death, Sooraj was awake much earlier than usual. He was washing a glass tumbler in the kitchen while I was preparing my morning tea. I suspect that he had mixed these tablets in the juice that Manimekhala had given him the previous evening because he had insisted that Uthra wanted some juice. I do not see that tumbler anywhere in the house now.'

'The tumbler would have helped us greatly in our investigation. We'll look for it, but whether we find it or not, we must use this piece of information once the matter is in court. We already know from the medical records at Pushpagiri that Uthra was sedated at the time of the first bite. A similar pattern is likely in the case of the second bite as well.'

'Sir, in March, Uthra had told Manimekhala that she used to feel giddy right after Sooraj served her porridge in the evenings. I think this was his plan all along, to drug her.'

'I will keep this in mind, Vijayasenan.'

The batch number on the Monty LC strip was traced back to the inventory of a medical store near Uthra's parents' house. The store's digital sales register had an entry which confirmed that the medicine had indeed been purchased by Sooraj.

Ashokan now came to the conclusion that the presence of both Sooraj and Suresh was essential to continue with the probe. He moved an application before the competent court for extending their custody, which was then granted on the basis of evidence that unmistakably indicated their involvement in the heinous offence. He was permitted to keep them in police custody till 4 June.

In their next meeting, the SIT recognised the need to put together an expert committee under Section 45 of the Indian Evidence Act[24] that could attest to the behavioural patterns and scientific facts related to snakes. Subsequently, a three-member expert committee was formed, comprising Dr K. Sasikala, the head of department of Forensic Medicine, Government Medical College Hospital, Mavish Kumar, a herpetologist, and Dr Kishore Kumar, the veterinary surgeon from the Animal Husbandry Department.

The SIT also evaluated the available material evidence and concluded that another inspection of Sooraj's residence was in order. Accordingly, the team conducted the search on 1 June at Parakkodu.

During this search, Ashokan seized an album bearing pictures of Sooraj and Uthra's marriage ceremony. Out of curiosity, he turned a few pages of the album and found himself unable to suppress a feeling of poignancy as he saw the innocent face of the young bride in the photographs. He tried to read Sooraj's face as well and concluded that the young man had displayed no visible

[24] 'When the Court has to form an opinion upon a point of foreign law or of science, or art, or as to identity of handwriting, or finger impressions, the opinions upon that point of persons specially skilled in such foreign law, science or art, or in questions as to identity of handwriting or finger impressions are relevant facts. Such persons are called experts.' (Section 45 of Indian Evidence Act)

signs of what he would turn out to be: a scheming and ruthless killer. Another proof of the wedding was a CD which was also collected as an exhibit. While he was collecting these exhibits, Ashokan also picked up another document which underlined the brutality that accompanied the cold-blooded murder—Uthra's disability certificate.

An Okacet tablet strip was also recovered during this search. Ashokan knew about the tablet as it had once been prescribed to him for relief from a bout of allergic itching. He recalled that it had some side effects such as blurred vision, depression, drowsiness, and agitation owing to one of its ingredients—cetirizine salt. This fell in line with what Vijayasenan had suspected about Uthra's sedation during the first attempt on her life. However, as things had turned out in that first attempt, the sedative mixture that had been given to Uthra had not proved potent enough to knock her unconscious.

The mobile phones of Sooraj's parents and his sister were collected to analyse if they had any links to the crime. Their interest, if not an active participation in the commission of the crime, could not have been ruled out.

The key to the locker that Uthra and Sooraj had maintained in the Adoor branch of the Federal Bank was seized too. The pages in the locker register of the bank where transactions were entered were photocopied and made part of the investigation process. Ashokan also managed to access the pledge card and the loan application documents that pertained to a gold loan that Sooraj had availed from the bank. He also seized a motor cycle which belonged to Sooraj.

Ashokan's next stop was at Suresh's house. He took possession of the van in which Suresh had transported the Russell's viper in March and the Honda Activa scooter which he had used to transport the cobra to the spot near Ajeem's pan shop where he had met Sooraj. On being questioned by Ashokan's team, Ajeem had confirmed that he had seen Suresh ride the scooter on the day which the SIT had zeroed in on as the day the murder weapon had exchanged hands.

The duration of police custody for the suspects was expiring on 4 June. With much ground still left to cover, Ashokan moved another application for extending the custody period and based on the compelling evidence already collected, the court granted another extension lasting till 8 June.

During the extended period of custody, the accused was taken to his residence at Parakkodu where he picked out the bedsheet on which Uthra had been lying and the nightgown and skirt that she had been wearing when she was bitten by the Russell's viper. Ashokan noted that Sooraj's body language showed no signs of remorse. These exhibits were all numbered and added to the existing pool of evidence. Later, the DNA recovered from the bedsheet, the nightgown, and the skirt was analysed. A female's DNA was found on the nightgown and the skirt. On further analysis, the DNA was found to be a perfect match for Uthra which incontrovertibly proved that these pieces of clothing belonged to her.

'Snakebite cases are rare in the area,' was an assertion by Dr Shahirsha who was the superintendent of the Taluk Hospital, Punalur. This was an authoritative statement made on the strength of official records and it was echoed by other medicos serving in the area. Sister Lilly Thomas, the director of St. Joseph's Mission Hospital, Anchal, Dr Rajkafoor, the superintendent of the Taluk Hospital, Kadakkal, Dr Prasanth T., the superintendent of Adoor General Hospital, and Dr Shemeer Salam, a doctor at the Anchal Community Health Centre, all confirmed Dr Shahirsha's assertion basis their own records.

Speaking about the venomous snakebite that Uthra had suffered from, Sister Alphiya, the administrator of Holy Cross Hospital, Adoor, told the police that in the past five years it had been the only case of a venomous snake being involved out of the fifteen snakebite cases that had been reported from Parakkodu.

It could be said with complete confidence that these statements, all made by staff members belonging to different hospitals, confirmed that Uthra being bitten by a Russell's viper and later a cobra was a matter which deserved to be deeply probed before any conclusions could be drawn about it being a natural occurrence. The SIT added these medical professionals to their list of expert witnesses.

The forest department also cooperated throughout the investigation. Their records were examined by Ashokan's team to gather an idea about the snake population in the Anchal area. Dinesh R., a section forester in the Konni Forest Division, testified that the jurisdiction of the Konni Wildlife Division extends over Pathanamthitta and the areas of Neendakara to Oachira in Kollam district. A striking force is maintained in the department to rescue wild animals which occasionally stray into human habitats. The details of the rescued animals are entered in a register. A perusal of the register showed that in the period between 2016 to 2020, no venomous snakes were rescued from the Parakkodu region. This highlighted the improbability of repeated bites by highly venomous snake species.

The Uthra case had grabbed the attention of not just the people of Anchal and Kollam areas, but it was also the talking point in the entire state of Kerala. The immense public interest in the case was multiplied by the wide coverage it received in both print and electronic media, with channels like Manorama, Mathrubhoomi, Asianet, and News18 among many others, covering the developments in the case extensively.

Sooraj was taken to his residence by Ashokan's team on 14 July. They were also accompanied by officials of the Forest Department. Bidin M. Das, a reporter of Asianet News, Pathanamthitta, went to cover this visit. When the team of investigators and Sooraj were about to leave, he asked Sooraj whether he had committed the offence or not. Much to his and everyone else's surprise, Sooraj replied in the affirmative. To add to the surprise, when a media person from Mathrubhoomi asked the accused whether he had committed the crime alone or with an accomplice or two, Sooraj said that no other person was involved in the offence.

Later, on the instructions of Hari Sankar, Mahesh Mohan rushed to Mathrubhoomi's office at Thiruvananthapuram and obtained the footage of Sooraj's confession. Some of the newspersons who had interviewed Sooraj also became entrants in the police's witness list now.

Uthra's post-mortem was conducted by Dr Ragesh R. The photographs taken during the examination showed a significant bluish discolouration of her skin. This indicated a high degree of envenomation which invariably leads to intolerable pain. It would be unnatural for a person to not seek immediate help in such a scenario. The delay in Uthra receiving medical aid pointed to her being possibly sedated at the time of the bite. The doctor also noted the presence of two ante-mortem injuries—two puncture wounds, each on the back of the left forearm, the punctures being 2.3 cm and 2.8 cm apart respectively. He concluded that the puncture wounds were consistent with snakebites, but found the bites to be unusual because they were in close proximity and the variance in the fang width of both was sizeable. Based on the minimal infiltration of blood by the venom and the tissue reaction around the bite marks, he also concluded that the snake was probably a cobra.

An assistant examiner in a chemical examiner's laboratory received samples of Uthra's blood, stomach, intestine, liver, kidney, and subcutaneous tissue after the preliminary examination by Dr Ragesh R. at the Government Medical College Hospital was done. She detected cobra venom in the blood and in the subcutaneous tissue of the bite site. Traces of cetirizine were found in the stomach, intestine, liver, kidney, and bloodstream. Uthra's blood contained 0.542 mg of cetirizine per

100 ml, which is much higher than the normal dosage prescribed for adults by medicos.

The primary cause of death listed in the post-mortem report was cobra envenomation. The report also underlined the presence of a non-therapeutic dose of cetirizine in Uthra's blood. This spoke to Uthra's sedated state at the time of the fatal bite and it could also be directly linked to the empty strip of Monty LC tablets that had been recovered from Sooraj's Baleno. The doctor also made a note about Uthra's low intelligence quotient, observing that her brain weighed 720 gm as opposed to the normal weight of an adult brain that ranges from 1,250 to 1,350 gm.

Both Ragesh R. and the chemical examiner were added to the witness list by the SIT.

It is relevant to note here that in 1984, the Supreme Court enumerated guidelines to establish murder by administration of poison. It laid down the requirement of four conditions for recording a conviction:

(i) There was a clear motive for the accused to administer poison to the deceased, (ii) the deceased died of the poison said to have been administered by the accused, (iii) the accused had the poison in his possession, and (iv) he had an opportunity to administer the poison to the deceased.[25]

[25] Sharad Birdhichand Sarda vs State of Maharashtra, AIR 1984 SC 1622.

The SIT had collected heaps of material and circumstantial evidence by now that satisfied all four of the conditions listed by the apex court. They even had a thorough post-mortem report that backed their case and an extrajudicial confession by the accused on record. However, the challenge to bring it all together as an impregnable story for a court of law was still a daunting task. The likelihood of Sooraj pleading guilty in court was negligible, and his lawyers would make every effort to get the extrajudicial confession thrown out from the list of permissible evidence. For special public prosecutor Mohan Raj, the task of ensuring that Uthra got justice against all these odds, was going to be onerous.

By July, a basic framework for the prosecution's case had been laid. The list of prosecution witnesses, while impressive in terms of qualifications and profiles, lacked a trump card that could be used to nail the crime on either Sooraj or Suresh. And in spite of all the evidence that the SIT had already gathered, Mohan Raj was adamant that both the accused would go scot-free.

'This is not going to be enough!' Mohan Raj exclaimed in frustration. He was closeted with Ashokan in a small chamber at the district court to discuss the way forward.

'I agree, but this is all we have,' Ashokan answered.

'There is always a new perspective to explore, my friend.'

'I wish real cop work actually resembled crime dramas. Just a proclamation of guilt by the ACP and the end credits roll.'

'*Tumko to phansi hi hogi,* you will be hanged!' Mohan Raj added and laughed loudly as he imitated the famous wrist movement of ACP Pradyuman.[26] Raj's broken Hindi accent added to the humour.

'The public must think we are jokers to be taking so long in what appears to be a cut-and-dried matter,' Ashokan said, still wearing a smile.

'Jokers? Yes. We need the joker in the pack.'

Ashokan gave his colleague a bemused look.

'Let's add Suresh to our side of the deck. He should be a witness for the prosecution.'

'What?' Ashokan sounded surprised.

'See, he knows the whole crime intimately and his testimony will definitely catch Sooraj's lawyers off guard. Suresh's direct involvement in the crime was in the capacity of an unwilling accomplice and we should exploit that angle. We need to offer him a plea deal.'

'Is that possible?'

'It has been done in some other cases. The co-accused becomes an approver in the case under Section 306.[27] The process involves recording a 164 statement[28] in front a judicial magistrate that holds enough promise to nail the perpetrator.'

---

[26] The top cop in the popular TV show *CID* which aired on Sony Entertainment Television from 1998–2018.

[27] A section in the Criminal Procedure Code dealing with the procedure for turning an accomplice in a crime to a witness for the prosecution. Such a witness is called an 'approver'.

[28] A witness statement recorded by a magistrate which holds greater evidentiary value in a court of law than Section 161 statements which are recorded by the police.

Ashokan started to pace up and down the cramped room. He had a spring in his step. He knew that this idea was a potential game changer.

'You should consult your superiors, Ashokan,' Mohan Raj advised.

'I will have a word with Suresh first! Thanks, Mohan Raj. I must get to work on this.'

'*Pata karo,* Daya, find out,' Mohan Raj quipped, easing the mood just as Ashokan was leaving, and both the men laughed heartily.

1 TO 4

'Omission is a sin only if, in the process of deceiving, you forget the truth. Lying is a sin only if, in the process, the lie becomes the only truth.'

–Julianna Baggott

Investigation is the natural step to follow after a crime is brought to the notice of the police. The fundamental philosophy which guides our law on who-done-it is for everyone to let the police do its job of investigation, and any interference in this activity is frowned upon. Even the courts of law are expected to remain aloof and not hold the hand of the sleuth duly appointed for the purpose of carrying out an investigation as per the provisions laid down in the books, especially the Code of Criminal Procedure (CrPC). The Supreme Court has clearly spelt out that an 'investigation must proceed unhampered by court orders.'[29] It has held that '...the legal position is absolutely clear and also settled by judicial authorities that the court

[29] Union of India vs Prakash P. Hinduja & Anr on 7 July 2003. (https://indiankanoon.org/doc/767596/).

would not interfere with the investigation or during the course of investigation.'[30] It has clarified that from the time of the lodging of the First Information Report till the submission of the report by the officer in charge of the police station in court is a function exclusively reserved for the investigating agency. It goes on to add in the same judgment that investigation 'is a clear-cut and well demarcated sphere of activity in the field of crime detection and crime punishment. Investigation of an offence is the field exclusively reserved for the executive through the police department....' The apex court states emphatically that, '...the executive is charged with a duty to keep vigilance over law and order' and is, therefore, responsible to prevent crime. So, if an offence is alleged to have been committed, it is its duty to investigate into the offence. Once the state finds that an offence has been committed, it is its obligation to collect evidence for the purpose of proving the offence. On completion of the probe, 'the investigating officer submits a report to the court requesting the court to take cognisance of the offence, its duty comes to an end.'[31]

Section 161 of the CrPC[32] is the vital provision establishing the manner in which a witness may be examined by a police

---

[30] Ibid.

[31] Ibid.

[32] Section 161 of the Code of Criminal Procedure, 1973—Examination of witnesses by the police:

(1) Any police officer making an investigation under this Chapter, or any police officer not below such rank as the State Government may, by general or special order, prescribe in this behalf, acting on the requisition of such officer, may examine orally any person

officer in the course of an investigation. It is laid down in the subsequent section that the signing of statements so recorded is prohibited. It is thought that if such statements are accepted as evidence, then police officers are likely to use strong-arm tactics in an unbridled manner, and for this reason the torture of suspects would become the rule. Whatever Sooraj, Suresh, and all the other witnesses told the SIT during the process of questioning would be governed under this provision.

Section 164 of the CrPC[33] provides for the recording of a witness' statement by a metropolitan or judicial magistrate. This statement is recorded after an assurance to the witness

---

supposed to be acquainted with the facts and circumstances of the case.

(2) Such person shall be bound to answer truly all questions relating to such case put to him by such officer, other than questions the answers to which would have a tendency to expose him to a criminal charge or to a penalty or forfeiture.

(3) The police officer may reduce into writing any statement made to him in the course of an examination under this section; and if he does so, he shall make a separate and true record of the statement of each such person whose statement he records.

33 Section 164 of the Code of Criminal Procedure, 1973—Recording of confessions and statements:

(1) Any Metropolitan Magistrate or Judicial Magistrate may, whether or not he has jurisdiction in the case, record any confession or statement made to him in the course of an investigation under this Chapter or under any other law for the time being in force, or at any time afterwards before the commencement of the inquiry or trial: Provided that no confession shall be recorded by a police officer on whom any power of a Magistrate has been conferred under any law for the time being in force.

that he or she has the right to refuse to record such a statement and that it is a voluntary act; it is also spelled out clearly

---

(2) The Magistrate shall, before recording any such confession, explain to the person making it that he is not bound to make a confession and that, if he does so, it may be used as evidence against him; and the Magistrate shall not record any such confession unless, upon questioning the person making it, he has reason to believe that it is being made voluntarily.

(3) If at any time before the confession is recorded, the person appearing before the Magistrate states that he is not willing to make the confession, the Magistrate shall not authorise the detention of such person in police custody.

(4) Any such confession shall be recorded in the manner provided in Section 281 for recording the examination of an accused person and shall be signed by the person making the confession; and the Magistrate shall make a memorandum at the foot of such record to the following effect: 'I have explained to (name) that he is not bound to make a confession and that, if he does so, any confession he may make may be used as evidence against him and I believe that this confession was voluntarily made. It was taken in my presence and hearing, and was read over to the person making it and admitted by him to be correct, and it contains a full and true account of the statement made by him.'

(Signed) A. B. Magistrate.

(5) Any statement (other than a confession) made under sub-section (1) shall be recorded in such manner hereinafter provided for the recording of evidence as is, in the opinion of the Magistrate, best fitted to the circumstances of the case; and the Magistrate shall have power to administer oath to the person whose statement is so recorded.

(6) The Magistrate recording a confession or statement under this section shall forward it to the Magistrate by whom the case is to be inquired into or tried.

that if he or she does get the statement recorded, it may be used as evidence against him or her. For instance, Suresh's statement about turning into an approver would fall under this provision.

But why is there a difference in tenor between the provisions prescribed for the police and those prescribed for a magistrate? Clearly, the CrPC, which was originally enacted way back in 1861, took into account the fact that a witness may be coerced into making statements under duress by the police while a magistrate is likely to command enough trust for the statement to be unsullied by similar factors. When the revised version of the CrPC was enacted in 1973, these provisions were retained because even after twenty-five years of independence, there was a large degree of distrust in the methods used by police investigators.

It is in this context that Section 25 of the Indian Evidence Act[34] also needs to be understood. This section renders confessions made before a police officer inadmissible in a trial before a court of law. For this reason, Sooraj's confession to Ashokan was not included in the case built by the prosecution.

The provision of Section 164 of the CrPC brings to the investigator the opportunity to not only get a signed statement from the accused, but it also adds to the confidence of the prosecution agency to achieve success. The objective of recording witness' statements under Section 164 of the code is twofold:

---

[34] Section 25 of the Indian Evidence Act, 1872—Confession to police officer not to be proved:
No confession made to a police officer shall be proved as against a person accused of any offence.

(i) to deter witnesses from changing their version of events at the trial for fear of being hauled up for perjury, and (ii) to get over the cloak of immunity ensured due to the non-admissibility of information given by the witnesses to the police.

When it comes to the question of whether there is a significant difference in the authenticity that Section 164 brings to a trial or not, the Patna High Court has held that the difference between a statement made before the police under Section 161 of the CrPC and that made under Section 164 of the CrPC before a magistrate is that the latter one is on oath and the witness is liable to face legal proceedings should he/she resile from the recorded statement. Fundamentally therefore, the quality of evidence does not undergo a change, only the method of recording it does, so does its admissibility. The magistrate enjoys an exalted position under law, and leaves the police officer investigating a crime far behind in this aspect. Significantly, as per protocol, the magistrate is approached by the investigating officer to record a statement under Section 164 when a witness expresses a readiness to do so. The magistrate does not do it on his own accord as a rule. Even when a witness pleads to have his or her statement recorded, such a request is generally not accepted by a magistrate.[35]

The statements made under Section 161 serve the purpose of putting up the findings of an investigating officer before the court at the time of admitting the case. They also help in framing the charges against the accused. During the trial, these

---

[35] Patna High Court – Mohd. Manir vs State of Bihar and Ors on 13 September 1994. Equivalent citations: 1994 (2) BLJR 1433.

statements are used for the purpose of underlining contradictions and omissions.

Omissions and contradictions relate to previous statements made by witnesses. When a witness misses stating something from the earlier statement at the trial, it amounts to what is called an omission. A contradiction is when a witness states something which is different from his or her earlier statement. Omissions and contradictions lead to an erosion of confidence in the evidence presented.

During the trial, a reference to 161 statements therefore offers to the prosecution the opportunity to question the testimony deposed by a witness and underline contradictions and omissions. The defence is also vigilant to pounce on anything that has even the slightest semblance of being either of these two.

Ashokan had before him the testimony of Suresh, and he saw just how beneficial Mohan Raj's idea would be to the prosecution's cause. Seeing the potential that the witness had, Ashokan got down to work and managed to convince Suresh to turn approver. The need to have Suresh's statement recorded by a magistrate under Section 164 came with two advantages—its reliability in a court of law would be enhanced and the likelihood of a retraction by the witness would be rendered faint.

At one stage during his interrogation by Ashokan, Sooraj, now the prime accused in this case, had admitted that he had killed Uthra. This statement, however, could not have been used in a court of law because it was hit by two provisions. One was that the Constitution prohibited the prosecution from bringing self-incriminatory statements made by an accused, and the other was the inadmissibility of statements made to police officers during an investigation.

One of the fundamental principles of jurisprudence is the provision of protection to an accused against self-incrimination. The right against self-incrimination is an essential fundamental right that cannot be taken away. Article 20(3) of the Indian Constitution articulates this right. It is significant that only an accused is given protection under Article 20(3). According to Sections 164 and 281 of the CrPC, only a magistrate can record a valid admissible confession. In fact, an extrajudicial confession is also admissible. The statement that Sooraj gave to a journalist about his guilt was indeed admitted in the trial. The credibility of confessional statements made to people other than police officers enjoys the sanctity of being admissible in a court of law.

It can therefore be surmised that the recording of statements under Sections 161 and 164 of the CrPC plays a pivotal role in a criminal trial. The purpose of there being a contradiction between the evidence provided by a witness before the court and the statement recorded under Sections 161 or 164 of the CrPC is not to shake the credibility of the witness, rather it is only to put the court on guard and get it to scrutinise the evidence presented by the witness with great care in the light of Section 145 of the Indian Evidence Act which deals with the aspect of contradictions.[36]

---

[36] Section 145 of the Indian Evidence Act, 1872—Cross-examination as to previous statements in writing:

A witness may be cross-examined as to previous statements made by him in writing or reduced into writing, and relevant to matters

After being run through all the levels of scrutiny, if the statements do not make a compelling story, it's usually because the witness has included elements of fiction. And so it is that almost every sharp lawyer believes in the popular Hindi idiom '*Jhooth bole kauaa kate* (speak a lie at your own peril)!'

---

in question, without such writing being shown to him, or being proved; but, if it is intended to contradict him by the writing, his attention must, before the writing can be proved, be called to those parts of it which are to be used for the purpose of contradicting him.

COILING AROUND

Jigsaw puzzles are fascinating to attempt. There may be hundreds and thousands of pieces which together complete the picture, but when it comes to the clinching piece, it is one that finds its fit only in the end. Should this one piece not sit where it ought to, the entire painstaking process of having worked on the puzzle becomes futile. Proving a crime incontrovertibly in a court of law is somewhat similar. The investigator and the pleading prosecutor may be right where the last bit is, but this small piece is also what the defence will pounce upon should the fit look even slightly out of place.

To create a credible crime scene for a court of law, the variables involved have to be minimised. The final perception that a judge has of the scene should be akin to a fingerprint—leaving little or no room for an alternate match. It becomes an almost obvious strategy for the defence to create scenarios which differ in detail from the version of the truth presented by the prosecutor. The presence of even the slightest thread of credibility in an alternate version of reality can lead to a big difference in the final sentencing.

The trial in the case of the State of Kerala vs Sooraj S. Kumar commenced on 1 December 2020. The trump card in the prosecution's deck of witnesses was played as the first hand. Suresh was produced in court as the first witness. He stuck to the statements he had made under Section 164 before the judicial magistrate, thereby providing the court with the kernel of truth. The training that he had been given by the SIT and the numerous sessions of mock cross-examination by Mohan Raj also paid off. Suresh stuck to the principle of speaking only what was essential during the cross-examination. He did not add any extra details or flourishes to his answers. The whole story was presented before the judge much like the chapters of a well-written book. Now, only some bits had to be fleshed out and a few anticipated variables had to be dealt with in a manner which had been rehearsed.

The biggest variable in this case was the murder weapon. It had a beating heart of its own and was also infamously cold-blooded. The credibility of the prosecution's version of events depended heavily on the behaviour of the snakes that Sooraj had used to commit the crime. As often happens in an arena of facts, there was only one way to substantiate this element of the case: science.

The presentation of a demonstration involving live venomous snakes was rare for a court of law. Even this haloed temple of justice, desensitised as it was to murky tales of crime, was abuzz with anticipation about the proposed demonstration. The footage of the demonstration was going to be viewed on the court's monitor.

Only a few months earlier, the chief wild life warden had sanctioned the live demonstration to be carried out at the Arippa Forest Training Institute. The props required were minimal—a dummy that resembled Uthra in form and dimensions and a couple of deadly snakes.

The setup of Uthra's room was recreated down to the last detail for the demonstration, which was carried out on the night of 28 July 2020 in the presence of the investigating officer, the assistant conservator of forests, the tehsildar, and a police photographer.

Uthra's dummy was laid down on a cot and a piece of chicken was tied to its hand to act as bait. An Indian cobra was the snake of choice for the first leg of the demonstration. It was released from a container which had been strategically positioned on top of the dummy. At first, the snake gracefully slithered away and made no attempt to harm the dummy. This underlined the fact that the basic nature of the reptile was to avoid conflict. Then the cobra was deliberately provoked by the handlers present on site. For this, the entire arm of the dummy on which the bait was tied was detached and then used to continuously prod the snake, but the reptile only resorted to its usual defence mechanisms of hooding and hissing. It was only after a prolonged period of provocation that it eventually bit into the piece of chicken. This bite was recorded as the first natural bite. On further provocation, the cobra bit again. The fang width of the two bites was identical at 1.7 cm. This finding corresponded with the research conducted by the National

Centre for Biological Information which said that the average fang width ranges from 1 cm to 1.6 cm.

The next step in the live demonstration was to induce forced bites and measure the difference in fang widths between forced and natural bites. This is a process that involves a high degree of skill which only experienced snake wranglers possess. The expert handlers present on site now forced the cobra's head onto the dummy until two bites were induced. The fang width in this scenario had larger dimensions at 2 cm and 2.4 cm respectively. The fang widths on Uthra's corpse had been of larger dimensions too—2.3 cm and 2.8 cm. This established that the fang width of forcefully induced bites was notably more than that of natural bites.

A senior herpetologist who was closely involved in the Kerala Forest Department's snake rescue and habitation programmes, informed the court about the skeletal makeup of the cobra. He told the court that a snake's skull is an assembly of movable joints and when external pressure is applied to the head, the upper jaw, which is where the fangs are located, expands. This was the reason why induced snakebites were wider than natural ones.

Another demonstration was held on 5 August 2020. There were two major differences between this demonstration and the one held earlier. The first was the choice of bait which, in this case, was a dead rat tied to the leg of the dummy. The second was the choice of snake. A Russell's viper was used this time. This demonstration was a re-enactment of the first attempt that was made on Uthra's life.

When the snake was released, it did not bite the dead rat immediately. This was evidently due to the absence of any thermal radiation from the animal. It was only when a live rat was tied to the dummy's leg that the snake bit on it. The court was also informed that the venom of a Russell's viper is hemotoxic (has cardiovascular and/or haemostatic effects) as opposed to a cobra's venom which is neurotoxic (meaning, it acts on the central nervous system).

The variation in fang widths as observed in the video coupled with the nature of Uthra's symptoms lent credibility to the theory of the 'murder weapon' being an unwilling ally in both the unsuccessful and successful attempts on her life.

Another important piece of the puzzle for the investigators was to establish that the snake had not entered the room on its own. The spot where Uthra had been lying on the fateful night had already been indicated by other witnesses in the case. The absence of venomous snakes in the region had been confirmed by experts as well. What the SIT needed to do was to establish the inaccessibility of the location for the snake.

The first step was to eliminate the possibility of the cobra's entry from the windows in Uthra's room. The window on the northern side was 115 cm from the ground while the windows on the eastern side were all at a height of 122 cm from the ground. It has been scientifically proven that cobras can lift up to a third of their body off the ground. The snake in this case was 152 cm long. Therefore, it could only have managed a vertical lift of just over 50 cm. Therefore, the probability of the cobra using any of the windows to gain access to the room was negligible. There were also no trees next to any of the windows, so the serpent could not have slithered up a branch and slid into the room. Additionally, the cot on which Uthra was sleeping was not adjacent to any of the windows.

The second point of entry could have been the bathroom's ventilation. While the exhaust fan was at a safe height of 210 cm from the ground, a fixed PVC pipe ran along the wall of the house. Cobras have been known to climb up small trees in an effort to catch prey. However, the climb in question, that too without an apparent prey in sight would be highly unlikely. Also, the PVC pipe was just 2.5 cm in diameter which would make it nearly impossible for the snake to scale up its length. A herpetologist seconded this submission by the prosecution. The bathroom's drainage facility was also ruled out as it led to a fixed steel plate cover, in other words, a dead end.

The gap between the bolted main door of the room and the floor was just a couple of millimetres. There was virtually no possibility of a cobra having wriggled its way in from under the door. The room was, for lack of a more appropriate term, cobra-proof.

The prosecution further stated that the natural habitat of cobras was in dry areas. The crime scene, on the other hand, was located in a marshy area, and there was no history of cobras being rescued from its general vicinity. Also, during summers, which was when Uthra had been bitten, cobras are known to be active only early in the morning. Uthra being bitten by the snake late at night was clearly in defiance of an age-old behavioural pattern.

The first attempt on Uthra's life was of great significance in the chain of events that led to the eventual homicide. Since there were some blanks in the second half of the tragic story as far as pure evidence was concerned, the testimonies of all those involved in treating Uthra after the first snakebite were extremely vital.

A witness who could authoritatively testify about Uthra's plight had to be one of the doctors from the Pushpagiri Medical College Hospital who had treated her. For this purpose, the prosecution summoned Dr Mathew Pulikkan, the head of the Critical Care department at the hospital. Dr Bhuvaneswari, who had first tended to Uthra in the emergency ward, had transferred her to his care after noticing the repeated fluctuation in her vitals. The veteran doctor testified that Uthra had been brought to the emergency ward of the hospital on 3 March 2020. He had been the doctor on duty supervising her treatment. Uthra's condition had been extremely critical and her vitals had not been recordable.

An important exhibit that was submitted by the prosecution was Uthra's case sheet. It had an in-depth summary of the treatment protocols that Uthra underwent in the various departments of the medical college. Dr Mathew Pulikkan stayed true to the facts listed in the report and presented a detailed account of what had transpired.

When Uthra first reached the hospital, she was semi-conscious. Her body was in a state of shock and her blood pressure was plummeting. There were snakebite marks on her right leg. She was admitted to the emergency department without wasting any time. Since her symptoms were consistent with those of envenomation, she was administered polyvalent anti-venom.

Even after being administered medication, Uthra's condition continued to be critical. Her blood pressure was dangerously low. Her drowsiness also persisted. She was eventually shifted to the ICU, but the process of resuscitating Uthra was proving to be difficult. She was given antibiotics and an infusion of platelets and plasma.

A surgeon inspected Uthra's wounds from the snakebite for signs of compartment syndrome. This is a painful condition that occurs when pressure within muscles builds up dangerously. Such an increase in pressure can subsequently cause a decrease in the blood flow, which in turn prevents nourishment and oxygen from reaching the nerve and muscle cells. Acute compartment syndrome is a medical emergency, and without timely treatment, it can lead to permanent muscle damage. In Uthra's case, extensive damage was recorded.

A nephrologist looked into Uthra's kidney function and found clear signs of impairment. Seeing no other alternative, a blood transfusion was done. The administration of antibiotics continued.

On the following day, a limb-saving fasciotomy was performed to relieve the growing pressure around the snakebite since that had resulted in a loss of circulation.

Uthra's recovery was slow, but she was finally not in danger of losing any limbs because of the snakebite. She exhibited signs of myocarditis[37] for a few days before she was stable.

Uthra owed her life to the high quality of the medical attention she received at the medical college. Once fully conscious, she was unable to recall when the snake had bitten her. All she remembered was the absolutely unbearable pain which had woken her up in the pitch darkness of the night. She recalled telling Sooraj about the pain, but he had decided to defer taking her to a hospital for a substantial amount of time. All of this was duly recorded in the case sheet by the staff of the medical college.

Dr Cyril Joseph, the head of department of Plastic Surgery, was also listed as a witness. He had seen Uthra after the fasciotomy. He attested to the extensive tissue damage around the wound on her right leg. He described the debridement surgeries that were performed to remove the dead tissue around the wound. He also told the court about the excruciating nature and the extended period of Uthra's ordeal. By the time she was discharged, the wound on her right leg had healed substantially but her locomotive abilities had been severely compromised. She was advised to keep visiting the hospital for dressings when she was discharged on 22 April 2020. Strangely, however, Uthra did not attend her follow-up consultation in which her doctors were planning to make her walk.

---

[37] Myocarditis is an inflammation of the middle layer of the heart wall. A severe case of myocarditis can weaken the heart, which can then lead to heart failure, abnormal heartbeat, and in some cases, even sudden death.

Other aspects of the unsuccessful attempt on Uthra's life were also a crucial part of the body of evidence that the prosecution was building up.

Uthra's discharge summary from the hospital in Tiruvalla was indicative of a Russell's viper having bitten her. The bite mark was 20 cm above the right ankle. The hemotoxic venom of a Russell's viper leads to excruciating pain and the lack of response from the victim should have sounded an alarm.

The scene of the attempted murder was the first-floor bedroom in Sooraj's home in Parakkodu. A two-storey building, Sree Surya, was not surrounded by any tall vegetation, and the area where it was located was not the traditional habitat of Russell's vipers. A staircase in the hall on the ground floor of the house led to the first-floor landing. The first floor had a bedroom and a small sit-out. The bedroom in question had two windows.

Russell's vipers are non-climbers and do not climb up staircases or any kind of vegetation. For a Russell's viper to climb up through a window or a staircase in search of prey is unheard of. Reputed snake handler Vava Suresh testified to this fact as a prosecution witness. In over thirty years of work in the field, he had been bitten sixteen times by Russell's vipers and 340 times by cobras. Of these, only three Russell's viper bites and ten cobra bites had caused critical damage. Vava Suresh went on to describe for the court the harrowing experience of dealing with the repercussions of these snakebites. He said that any person who gets bitten by either of the two snakes is bound to react immediately. The fact that Uthra was bitten twice by a cobra but did not even wince could only be explained by her being in a deep state of sedation.

Vava Suresh's statement stood on firm grounds because of his own injuries. He had an amputated left middle finger owing to a cobra bite. He was also incapable of rotating his right wrist inwards due to tissue damage caused by another snakebite. Prosecutor Mohan Raj told the court that Vava Suresh wore these injuries as medals and that the court must consider them a certification of his experience. A living testament to the horrors of envenomation, Vava Suresh was certain that foul play was the cause of Uthra's demise. He said he had never known of a Russell's viper which had found its way to the first floor of a house. He had also visited Sooraj's neighbourhood after the incident and was told by the local people there that no Russell's vipers had been seen in the area for decades.

Vava Suresh also pointed out that he had rescued snakes on thirty occasions from Parakkodu, but none of them was a Russell's viper. In fact, only days prior to Uthra's death, he had rescued a non-venomous snake in the area. He said that Parakkodu had large estates and paddy fields where snakes would accidentally fall into canals.

He told the court that in any case of successive accidental bites, the fang width remains uniform. He added even more meat to the prosecution's case when he said that snakebites meant for self-protection are solitary. A snake will immediately escape from the spot after biting a potential enemy as an act of self-protection and would never risk harm at the hands of said enemy by lingering back for a second bite.

In spite of the injuries he had suffered, Vava Suresh's love for snakes was evident. He made it absolutely clear in his statement that a snake would never turn hostile without serious provocation. He also went on to express his views on the grave nature of Uthra's demise in a programme called *Snake Master* which was telecast on a prominent channel.

Building a good case involves admitting and justifying potential loopholes in the corpus of evidence presented before the defence can capitalise on them. The prosecution was aware that the report about the blood sample that had been collected from Uthra's corpse was a credible bone of contention. This had made Dr R. Radhakrishnan, the head of department of Laboratory Medicine and Molecular Diagnostics at the Rajiv Gandhi Centre for Biotechnology, Kariyavattam, a very important witness. However, he was introduced fairly late in the proceedings as a matter of strategy. More than seventy witnesses had already been examined before him.

The examination-in-chief[38] began with some routine questions which helped the witness ease into the process. During his statement, Dr Radhakrishnan cited a Government of India report that recorded 60,000 deaths caused by snakebites every year. This disturbingly high number of deaths had prompted the Department of Science and Technology to request the

[38] The statement made by a witness before the court. This is often followed by a cross-examination by the defence lawyer.

Rajiv Gandhi Centre for Biotechnology to develop a test that could identify the snake based on its venom. This project was completed in 2019.

Dr Radhakrishnan described how a lateral flow-based point-of-care device[39] was designed for this purpose. The functionality of the test is similar to that of a pregnancy test. Two drops of venom extracted from the bite are placed on the card and the number of lines that appear on the card indicate the type of snake the venom belongs to. The four major types of snakes that the test is capable of detecting are cobras, Russell's vipers, kraits, and saw-scaled vipers. The entire process takes all of five minutes to fetch a positive result. Negative results, on the other hand, take an agonising twenty minutes. This test, however, is meant only for diagnostic purposes and is not classified as a forensic tool.

Venom is a protein and it demands proper preservation. Its traces vanish from blood over a period of time in a phenomenon called autolysis, which is the destruction of a cell through the actions of its own enzymes. The forensic tool used for the detection of venom is micro-diffusion on immune-diffusion either from the tissue or the wound exudate around the bite.

In Uthra's case, the sample that had been sent for detecting the type of venom was two months old. While it was put through rigorous testing, both diagnostic and forensic, cobra venom had not been found in the sample. However, the witness clarified before the court that this did not mean that a cobra

---

[39] A paper-based diagnostic tool similar in function to a COVID or pregnancy home test.

had not been used for the attack on Uthra. According to him, the most probable cause for the non-detection was the delay in sending the sample and the fact that the traces of venom had already vanished from the deceased's blood by the time the sample had been collected. The sample that was being tested was far from ideal. It was, for all practical purposes, just blood.

While this testimony did not exactly solidify the prosecution's case, it definitely robbed the defence of a surprise act built on the absence of cobra venom in Uthra's corpse. The cross-examination of Dr Radhakrishnan was always going to be challenging, but the prosecution had given him firm ground to stand on. An admission of guilt, or in this instance delay, is sometimes an effective means of staying ahead of the eight ball.

Apart from the live demonstrations and all the testimonies by the experts the SIT and the prosecution had gathered, members of Uthra's family also recounted their version of events in the court as prosecution witnesses. They held strong through the testing cross-examinations too. At this stage, the defence must have seen the writing on the wall, but the prosecution still had other pieces of evidence up its sleeve.

INNOCENT UNTIL...

Truth has the dubious quality of being seen in different hues by different people. Seemingly foolproof cases crumble a lot more routinely than one would like to imagine. A good defence counsel always has a compelling alternative to present in court. And in spite of the thorough case presented by the prosecution, Sooraj's sentencing was still a distant thought. The defence was most certainly going to go on the offensive!

Questioning the credibility of key witnesses is a go-to strategy in cases where evidence is amassed based on circumstances and expert opinions. Even the slightest doubt in the mind of a judge can make a huge difference when it comes to the quantum of punishment awarded or even the proof of a crime.

The report of the expert committee which ruled out the possibility of the two snakes having accidentally bitten Uthra and which also spoke of the variance in fang widths was a key piece of evidence. Any question marks on the characters and qualifications of the members of the committee would be fatal to the prosecution's plea.

'Expert' is a term that often sits loosely on the people it is used for. When someone is presented as an expert in a court of law, the qualifications and the experience of that person must live up to this tall claim. Delegitimising expert opinions is a time-tested practice for defence lawyers. The verbal volleys involved in the process can get nasty, but scoring a point is all that matters!

Mavish Kumar was the sole herpetologist on the committee that had looked into Uthra's death. His observations were indispensable when it came to concluding the nature of Sooraj's diabolical plan. He was, therefore, bound to face music from the defence counsel.

In an attempt to establish the supposedly preposterous nature of the expert committee's report, the defence counsel went after Mavish Kumar's qualifications. The first line of argument was that Mavish was a self-proclaimed expert on snakes who had made exaggerated claims about his educational background. He had degrees in botany and earth sciences but none in herpetology specifically. There were no research papers to his credit and he was not a PhD scholar either. The defence also said that the guidance which Mavish apparently gave to MPhil and MSc students could not be substantiated.

Mavish had testified about the cobra's ability to gain a vertical lift equal to one-third of its length based on what he had read in books written by J. C. Daniel[40] and Vivek Menon.[41] The

[40] J. C. Daniel began his career with the Bombay Natural History Society as a curator. He then went on to become its first director, and continues his association with the Society even after his retirement as the honorary secretary.

[41] Vivek Menon is a reputed wildlife conservationist, serial entrepreneur in the not-for-profit sector, and the founder of the Wildlife Trust of India.

defence said that the witness was incapable of understanding the full meaning of what the authors had written. Additionally, the defence said that the witness had not relied on any bona fide text to make observations about the standard fang width of the cobra. His testimony was deemed superficial and misleading. It was presented as a major blot on the entire report tabled by the expert committee.

The defence counsel also said that the witness' claims of being the chief zoologist in a Dubai-based company were false. He added that the company was into designing water theme parks, a task which had little or no room for employing an expert in zoology. He also pointed out that the Mahindra Wildlife Foundation, of which Mavish Kumar was apparently the chairman, had been defunct since 2016.

The defence counsel then went on to argue that the prosecution should have examined a herpetologist trained at the Wildlife Institute[42] in Dehradun. He suggested that even an expert snake handler would find it difficult to induce snakebites, and this team of experts that had been gathered by the prosecution was grossly incompetent.

---

[42] The Wildlife Institute of India (WII), headquartered in Dehradun, is an autonomous natural resource service institution established in 1982 under the Ministry of Environment, Forest, and Climate Change. It carries out wildlife research in areas of study like biodiversity, endangered species, wildlife policy, wildlife management, wildlife forensics, spatial modelling, eco-development, ecotoxicology, habitat ecology, and climate change.

The strategy of the defence counsel was clear. The idea was to prove that the expert committee's report did not hold much water. This roadmap was obvious in terms of strategy, but it was irrefutably also the most effective.

The next witness whose statement was brought under the scanner by the defence counsel was Dr Kishore Kumar, who was a veterinary surgeon in the Animal Husbandry Department and a member of the prosecution's expert committee. He had conducted the necropsy on the exhumed cobra.

Conducting a post-mortem examination on the carcass of a snake is an incredibly delicate process. The slightest deviation from protocol or any missing links being spotted in the final report can derail the cause of an otherwise thorough investigation. Good sleuth work often draws upon the rich veins of information that a post-mortem throws up. When it comes to serpents, the necropsy provides critical data about the snake's morbidity and mortality.

Systematically conducted necropsies have some common characteristics—all relevant tissues are collected for evaluation and every conceivable effort is made to create a sterile environment. Any contamination of the tissue samples can skew the results and in effect, come in the way of delivering justice. After the contents of the coelom (the main body cavity in most animals) are extracted, the snake is submerged in formalin. If the snake is venomous, its head is carefully disarticulated before transferring the rest of its body to the formalin-filled container.

The snake in this case had been exhumed and several chunks of information had already been lost to the elements.

The challenge of creating a proper post-mortem report was tantamount to putting together the whole carcass again, one scale at a time.

The testimony of Dr Kumar had established that the cobra used for attacking Uthra had been deliberately starved by Sooraj. The defence now stated that this was a conscious move by the prosecution to only reveal a part of the truth. The wily lawyer stressed on the fact that an absence of food in the cobra's coelom could not be mistaken for starvation, and that snakes could survive without consuming food for months at a time.

Like Mavish Kumar, the veterinarian had also backed the theory about the inability of the two snakes to accidentally stumble into the scene of crime each time. The defence, however, continued to argue that the experts were unaware of the locomotive abilities that snakes possessed, and that the possibility of an entry from one of the eastern windows in Uthra's room could not be discounted.

The defence harped on Kishore Kumar's allegedly shallow knowledge base and said that his understanding of snakes was built on what he had read in elementary textbooks. Some renowned books on herpetology published across the world differed with his points of view. This argument was further expanded to say that the witness was not in a position to declare how the fang width of a cobra would change when external pressure was applied on its head.

The effort to dismantle the expert committee's credibility was the first of many moves made by the defence. The next step was to discredit the post-mortem examination of the deceased.

The witness who had conducted the autopsy was Dr Ragesh R. The defence began with the contention that he had deviated from standard protocol while conducting the post-mortem examination. This, according to the defence lawyer, was reflected by the absence of relevant details in the original report—specifically, the mention of a paralysed diaphragm, details regarding Uthra's orifices, and an observation about the lack of oedema (swelling) on the bite site.

The defence counsel went on to say that the overwriting in the detailed post-mortem notes indicated that several changes had been made as an afterthought to favour the kind of case the prosecution wanted to build up. And this was a dubious attempt to cover up the incompetence of the post-mortem itself.

Like other key witnesses, Dr Ragesh's competence was also questioned. He was accused by the defence of deliberately delaying the issuance of the post-mortem certificate in order to support whatever case the police built. The defence also argued that any post-mortem expert worth his salt would be able to see, even after a cursory examination, that the distance between the bites on Uthra's elbow indicated a fang width of more than 2.7 cm.

The best way to not crumble under the pressure of a cross-examination is to be armed with facts, and Dr Ragesh R. was certainly more than equal to the task.

He started by talking about his position at the hospital as a junior resident in the Department of Forensic Medicine. He had conducted as many as 600 post-mortem examinations in his career. He had either witnessed or participated in three snakebite cases before conducting the post-mortem examination on Uthra's corpse. He said that there was no rule which prescribed that the post-mortem report had to be submitted within three days. He claimed that the delay in issuing the post-mortem report in Uthra's case had only happened due to a strict adherence to protocol and an extremely tight work schedule.

The doctor then explained how neurotoxic venom first paralyses the nerves which leads to respiratory paralysis and then causes asphyxia. He said that after death, all the muscles in the victim's body become flaccid and then rigor mortis[43] sets in. He stated the obvious by saying that an ante-mortem (occurring or performed before death) paralysis of muscles could not have been confirmed in the post-mortem report. Uthra's diaphragm was intact in terms of its anatomical structure. Whether the diaphragm was paralysed or not could only be ascertained based on what the body of the deceased exhibited.

In Uthra's case, there were clear signs of asphyxia; there was obstruction of the normal flux of blood within the blood vessel network of internal organs and her brain had swelled up. Her lungs were not oedematous (abnormally swollen) as was clearly mentioned in the report prepared by him. He dismissed the insinuations of the defence counsel about oversight. He clarified that if Uthra's lungs had indeed been swollen, this fact would have found its way into the post-mortem report. He stated that lung oedema is not a customary sign of respiratory arrest after envenomation.

The defence asked Dr Ragesh R. a pointed question about hypoxia or respiratory paralysis not being mentioned as the cause

---

[43] Rigor mortis is one of the most recognisable signs of death. It is characterised by a stiffening of the corpse's limbs which is caused by chemical changes in the muscles post-mortem.

of death. To this the witness responded by saying that the cause of death is always the first event in the chain of events that led to the victim's demise. In this case, the initial event was irrefutably a snakebite.

The defence then suggested that the presence of fatty streaks in Uthra's aorta were reflective of a cardiac ailment. The witness countered this assertion by pointing out that these streaks were perfectly normal at Uthra's age. The defence lawyer cited a paragraph in the report about blood spreading into the surrounding tissues. Dr Ragesh R. dismissed the idea that this was suggestive of internal bleeding.

The defence said that Uthra's corpse should have exhibited pedal oedema (the accumulation of fluid in the feet and lower legs). This suggestion was immediately struck down by the doctor. He said that Uthra's death was caused due to respiratory paralysis after the cobra bite and that pedal oedema was not an essential symptom in instances of envenomation. He also explained that unlike the Russell's viper's venom, cobra venom does not directly impact the muscles.

While cross-examinations are usually nail-biting sagas, some witnesses handle them better than others. Witnesses who have the ability to think on their feet can sometimes turn the tables on the defence counsel. A medical professional with thorough knowledge is a double-edged sword. They can exhibit a tendency to speak too much and make mistakes. On the other hand, if he or she knows how to remain calm when the heat is on, every statement made can translate into some kind of evidentiary value. Dr Ragesh R. had excelled in his examination-in-chief by the prosecution. He had now also put the defence on the back foot.

Dr R. Radhakrishnan, the head of department of Laboratory Medicine and Molecular Diagnostics at Rajiv Gandhi Centre for Biotechnology, was a witness who had a large number of questions to answer. The case hinged on his ability to field difficult questions in the cross-examination.

Dr Radhakrishnan had already told the court about the point-of-care device which was used to identify the type of snake basis venom samples. The prosecution additionally asked him about the sensitivity, specificity, and life span of the lateral flow test. The doctor kept his calm. He drew a parallel with the lateral flow technique used for detecting COVID-19. He said that owing to the outbreak of the virus, a large amount of data was available to evaluate this type of testing on all parameters. The sensitivity and specificity data of the venom test stood at 50 per cent and 80 per cent respectively. He went on to say that this was the case when ideal samples were used. In Uthra's case, the sample received was two months old and far from the kind of sample which would meet the conditions for high sensitivity.

He was then grilled about the disparity between the chemical analysis report and the diagnosis of the snake venom. With the confidence of a seasoned veteran, he told the court about how both the tests were unrelated procedures with vastly different methodologies. The World Health Organisation (WHO) recognised the method of testing adopted by the Rajiv Gandhi Centre for Biotechnology as a point-of-care device.

He stated that venom does not usually find its way into urine samples since proteins have a positive charge as opposed to the negative charge of kidneys. Unless a person had a malfunctioning kidney, snake venom, a protein, would not be detected in a urine test. Therefore, the absence of venom in Uthra's urine was consistent with the other conclusions of the post-mortem.

He also said on record that the ELISA test was recognised as the only commercial diagnostic test for detecting snake venom.

The doctors who tended to Uthra after she had been bit by the Russell's viper were also cross-examined. Some important facts came to light during the process.

The twenty-minute whole blood clotting test (used as a bedside diagnostic test for coagulopathic snake envenoming) was done on Uthra. There was no need to carry out the ELISA test as Uthra exhibited all the telltale symptoms of envenomation. These symptoms included local swelling at the bite site, problems with blood coagulation, kidney dysfunction, and unmistakable bite marks. It was more than evident that the patient had been bitten by a highly venomous snake and that any delay in treatment could have proved to be fatal.

The live demonstrations done using the cobra and the Russell's viper made not just for thrilling viewing, but also underlined the mind-set of the murder weapons themselves. However, since this piece of evidence was highly unconventional, its admissibility was vehemently challenged by the defence. The court was requested by the defence to discard the demonstrations as they were unreliable. This move by Sooraj's lawyers would eventually lead to the citation of several landmark judgments delivered by the apex court in the final verdict.

DEFANGED

13 October 2021

'This is a case of diabolic and ghastly uxoricide, committed stealthily, by inflicting induced cobra bites causing fatal envenomation, with extreme wickedness, to disguise it as death due to accidental cobra bite.'

These were the strongly worded opening lines of the judgment delivered by the Kollam trial court in Case No. 820/2020 State of Kerala vs Sooraj S. Kumar. The court held that the murder was 'diabolic, ghastly, brutal, and heinous,' and that the 'offence was committed with unparalleled wickedness and in a ghastly manner.'

Sooraj was found guilty under Sections 302 (Murder), 307 (Attempt to murder), 328 (Causing hurt by means of poison), and 201 (Destruction of evidence) of the IPC. Double life imprisonment was awarded in the first two sections and seventeen years in jail under the last two sections. The life terms for the murder and the attempt to murder would start only after Sooraj had been in prison for seventeen years (ten for poisoning his wife and seven for destruction of evidence). Sooraj was also directed to pay a fine of Rs 5,85,000.

Uthra's parents told the media that they were unhappy with the verdict as they had expected a death sentence.

'Capital punishment would have given a clear message to people who have such criminal minds,' Manimekhala told the *Hindustan Times*.[44]

Sooraj has since filed an appeal in the Kerala High Court against the orders of the Kollam trial court.

During the course of the investigation into Uthra's murder, thirty-eight gold sovereigns, which were a part of the dowry that Sooraj had received, were dug out by the sleuths from a rubber plantation to the east of Sooraj's house. Uthra's father-in-law, Surendran Panicker, was arrested after the recovery of these sovereigns. Sooraj, Surendran, S. Renuka (Uthra's mother-in-law), and Uthra's sister-in-law are facing a separate trial under the dowry prohibition and domestic violence acts.[45]

The custody of Uthra and Sooraj's son, Dhruv, was granted to his maternal grandparents Vijayasenan and Manimekhala. While he is growing up in the loving care of doting grandparents, Dhruv has to deal with the tainted shadow of his father for the rest of his life.

---

44 'Kerala snake bite case: Man gets double life sentence for murdering wife,' the *Hindustan Times*.

45 'Kerala snake-bite murder case: Two more arrested, police interrogates victim's mother-in-law,' *Mumbai Mirror*, www.indiatimes.com

Suresh, by virtue of being an approver in the criminal case against Sooraj, did not receive any punishment for supplying the snakes. However, the case which had been lodged against him under the Wild Life (Protection) Act is still being tried. He is currently out on bail and is living with his wife and daughter.

Interestingly, just days before the decision in the Uthra murder case, on 6 October, a bench of three judges of the Supreme Court had denied bail to two accused persons because of the new trend of snakes being used as murder weapons. In the case in question, it was alleged that a woman, her paramour, and a snake charmer were involved in a conspiracy to murder her mother-in-law. There too, the snake charmer who had supplied the snake was made an approver in the case.[46]

[46] 'Snake a deadly murder weapon, SC denies bail to two,' the *Times of India.*

BEYOND REASONABLE DOUBT

The games that are played in courts of law across the globe make for fascinating viewing. How statements, words, or even punctuations can take a story into the most unexpected of lanes that lead to destinations no one had ever thought of are the products of these games. A twist in the tale is what makes a story fascinating, and if the straightest of them appear to be a bundle of intricate coils, it is often because lawyers come with an unearthly ability to bring in elements of surprise.

What is presented before the person dressed in black robes sitting on an elevated seat with a white curly wig atop his or her head and appearing to be a repository of all wisdom is the material without which even the best-known secrets remain unproved.

The law which governs one of the most important aspects of a case, which is the admissibility of evidence in the courts of India, is the Indian Evidence Act which came into being in the year 1872. In its existence spanning a century and a half, this Act has seen very minor changes, thanks to court rulings, and has mostly stood strong with its fundamentals nearly unscathed.

Facts lead to conclusions which have different labels. For instance, something is 'proved' when the court, after considering the evidence brought before it, 'either believes it to exist, or considers its existence so probable that a prudent man ought, under the circumstances of the particular case, to act upon the supposition that it exists.'[47]

Another label is 'disproved'. The Evidence Act says that, 'A fact is said to be disproved when, after considering the matters before it, the court either believes that it does not exist, or considers its non-existence so probable that a prudent man ought, under the circumstances of the particular case, to act upon the supposition that it does not exist.'

A third category is 'not proved'. Simply stated, 'A fact is said not to be proved when it is neither proved nor disproved.'

Then there are those facts which the court 'may presume', as in 'the court may presume a fact, it may either regard such fact as proved, unless and until it is disproved, or may call for proof of it.'

Another category is 'shall presume', which means that, 'whenever it is directed by this Act that the Court shall presume a fact, it shall regard such fact as proved, unless and until it is disproved.'

And, finally, 'conclusive proof'—'When one fact is declared by this Act to be conclusive proof of another, the court shall, on proof of the one fact, regard the other as proved, and shall not allow evidence to be given for the purpose of disproving it.'

Clearly, all these options bring in multitudes of interpretations and provide to champion jugglers opportunities

---

[47] The Indian Evidence Act, 1872.

to skilfully manipulate presentations. The ones with the genius to exploit these niceties of law are the most successful of lawyers.

Evidence has its varieties based on whether someone actually saw something happening, or there are circumstances which lead the court to accept conclusions presented before it by the lawyers. Circumstantial evidence is 'that wonderful fabric which is built out of straws collected at every point of the compass, and which is yet strong enough to hang a man.'[48]

Circumstantial evidence, however, has often been looked upon as the poor cousin of what is called direct evidence. Courts place a greater emphasis on this second kind of evidence. Direct evidence may be both oral or documentary. The person who has actually seen the accused in a case attack the victim of a murder with the murder weapon will be readily accepted as a person who is aware of what happened, leaving little scope to sweep away his or her testimony as unreliable. Even in instances of such direct evidence being presented, the credibility of the witness, however, is an issue which the opposing lawyer will question. The fact is that even after taking the oath to speak only the truth, there are some witnesses who commit perjury. A document is, likewise, something that is before the judge and, save for reasons of its doubtful authenticity, will rarely be overlooked.

Direct evidence may, however, be inadequate in telling a story to its fullest. No loopholes can be left for the opposition to pounce upon for disproving a story. For the prosecution, it is always a challenging task to present a story that is so foolproof that the defence is unable to find even minor

---

[48] *Lady Audley's Secret* by Mary Elizabeth Braddon.

missing links in it. It must be like an impregnable wall in which there isn't a single brick which is weak and the cement which glues all the bricks together is, likewise, unassailable. Looking at this simile, one cannot help but appreciate the great importance of the cement in the wall, which, in this case, is the circumstantial evidence. It would be hard to find any successfully tried cases where circumstantial evidence has not been the link that makes the prosecution's entire story invincible and incorruptible.

Interestingly, there are a number of cases in which just circumstantial evidence has led to a conviction. The apex court has, however, placed a number of conditions for circumstantial evidence to be considered admissible, reliable, and sufficient enough to lead to a conviction. These conditions are:

(i) The circumstances from which the conclusion of guilt is to be drawn should be fully established. The circumstances concerned 'must' or 'should,' and not 'may' be established;
(ii) The facts so established should be consistent only with the hypothesis of the guilt of the accused, that is to say, they should not be explainable on any other hypothesis except that the accused is guilty;
(iii) The circumstances should be of a conclusive nature and tendency;
(iv) They should exclude every possible hypothesis except the one to be proved; and
(v) There must be a chain of evidence so complete as not to leave any reasonable ground for the conclusion consistent with the innocence of the accused and must

> show that in all human probability the act must have been done by the accused.[49]

One can see the enormous amount of work required of the prosecution to prove the guilt of an accused when circumstantial evidence is all they have. The investigating officers have to strain to the last of their capabilities and toil to come up with what is an unassailable conclusion. For, as the irrepressible Mark Twain says, 'Even the clearest and most perfect circumstantial evidence is likely to be at fault, after all, and therefore ought to be received with great caution. Take the case of any pencil, sharpened by any woman; if you have witnesses, you will find she did it with a knife; but if you take simply the aspect of the pencil, you will say she did it with her teeth.'[50]

Sir Arthur Conan Doyle, the creator of numerous great crime fiction stories, also points to the nature of circumstantial evidence being slippery and capable of being interpreted differently by different people. He says, 'Circumstantial evidence is a very tricky thing. It may seem to point very straight to one thing, but if you shift your own point of view a little, you may find it pointing in an equally uncompromising manner to something entirely different.'[51]

Circumstantial evidence is indeed a tricky thing, as Sir Arthur Conan Doyle said. This is amply illustrated by a murder trial which occurred in district Shahjahanpur, Uttar Pradesh, where

---

[49] Sharad Birdhichand Sarda vs State of Maharashtra, AIR 1984 SC 1622.

[50] *Pudd'nhead Wilson* by Mark Twain

[51] Arthur Conan Doyle, *The Adventures of Sherlock Holmes.*

Aloke Lal, the co-author of this book, was heading the district police as its superintendent. Information was brought to the *kotwali* (police station) by a resident of a congested locality about a house which was locked from the outside and from which a fetid smell was emanating. Things were so bad, said the resident, that it was nearly impossible for the neighbouring residents to breathe.

An officer was rushed to the location to investigate. He asked the people in the neighbourhood about the identity of the family which lived in the house, but not many came forward with any useful leads. However, the grocer across the road from the house, a man named Hanuman, said, 'I know the man who lives here. He had moved into this house a few weeks back. He buys his groceries from my shop. When I conversed with him, I found that he is not an easy man to draw out, though he could be communicative enough when the mood seizes him.'

'Well?' the police officer looked at him quizzically, 'What mood?'

'He was fond of his evening tipple. He would sit on the *takht* (sofa) outside when he drank. He would often call me over to accompany him. I myself do not drink, but he appeared to be mysterious in his ways, and I wanted to unravel what lay behind the shifty gaze of this reclusive loner. So I would go over and sit with him. I wondered why he rarely, if ever, looked straight at me when talking…'

'So, you do not know who this man was?' the policeman demanded.

'No, he never told me his real name. When I asked him about his identity, all he said was, "What will you do by knowing who

I am? Call me Munna, if you must address me by a name." That is all I know about him.'

'Hmm…I take it that he lived alone?'

'Yes, sir. In the first few weeks after he moved here, Munna lived alone, but a few days back he came here with a woman. I presumed that she is his wife.'

'What are the chances that you can trace him out?'

'All I know is that he used an old Bullet motorcycle. I remember the registration number. Maybe that can help? The number is UPN 9753. The numerals are odd numbers in descending order, sir. That's how I remember this; numbers fascinate me.'

The police officer called the constable accompanying him and gave the man some instructions. He then went through the usual protocol for breaking open the locked door of the house, and as expected, there was a dead body inside. It was a woman who appeared to be in her early thirties.

The body of the woman was sent for a post-mortem examination. Other physical evidence was collected from the scene by the investigating officer. There were no indications at all that anyone other than Munna had come into the house. The woman had also not been seen by anyone in the locality. Hanuman was the only one who had seen her, that too briefly, when Munna had driven her over to the house on his bike. She never came out of the house while she had lived in it.

The investigating officer thought out aloud, 'It seems like she was killed on the very day she came here.' From the degree of the body's decomposition this appeared to be the most likely possibility. The post-mortem report confirmed this impression too. It also established the cause of death: poison.

The case appeared to be a simple enough open-and-shut matter: the man called Munna had brought the deceased to his house. He had administered the poison, then locked the house from outside, and vanished from the scene.

The investigating officer only had the grocer Hanuman's word about who this Munna was. He was the only one from the locality who had had the opportunity to talk to the suspect. Hanuman told the police that during an interaction with Munna, when inebriation had compromised the latter's ability to keep his secrets to himself, Munna had said that he just could not tolerate unfaithfulness. He was of the view that those who cheat on their partners have lost their right to live.

In the meantime, the report from the Regional Transport Office (RTO) had been obtained. The number UPN 9753 was the number of a truck which had been seized from a transporter. It had not been allotted to a motorcycle. When the transporter was contacted, he confirmed that the truck with the stated number belonged to him and that it had been seized on charges of carrying drugs. It was found that the driver of the truck, a man named Kamala Prasad aka Munna, who had been employed by the transporter, was the culprit, and he was currently sought for the offence in another district where the drugs had been recovered by the police. The description of the man that Hanuman had given to the police matched the one provided by the transporter. The investigating officer got Munna's address from the transporter and began the process of tracking the man down. The accused was finally found close to the Nepal border, where he was planning to flee the country. In his statements, Kamala Prasad was evasive, and he refused to acknowledge that he was responsible for the murder of the woman.

In the court of law, the case was fought vigorously by the prosecutor. All the angles of the entire story were covered by the prosecution. The investigating officer and the SHO had worked day and night to build up a strong case and were completely justified in looking forward to a favourable judgment—that of Munna's conviction.

The defence lawyer, meanwhile, kept harping on the fact that no one had actually seen or heard anything suspicious while the accused and the victim were together inside the house. Why was it not possible that the woman herself had committed suicide? If the accused had indeed left the house on a certain day, why had no one seen him locking the house and leaving? Could someone else have found access into the house while the accused was not there and committed the crime?

One can see that while the investigators had painstakingly collected all the evidence, the defence was mostly offering arguments which amounted to little more than conjecture. Yet, doubts were raised. The possibilities pointed out by the defence counsel were primarily based on pulp fiction-like narratives, and their rebuttal, therefore, had to come in a strong manner based, ironically so, on direct evidence. But the prosecution's case, which everyone knew to be true, was based entirely on circumstantial evidence, and the defence had very successfully brought the ghost of reasonable doubt into the picture.

The apex court has acknowledged that the administration of poison with the intent to end a life is not an event for which witnesses are likely to be around. 'A case of murder by administration of poison is almost always one of secrecy. The poisoner seldom takes another into his confidence, and his preparations to the commission of the offence are also secret. He watches his opportunity and administers the poison in a manner calculated to avoid its detection. The greater his knowledge of poisons, the greater (is) the secrecy, and consequently the greater the difficulty of proving the case against him.'[52]

One cannot but believe in Aldous Huxley when he says, 'Facts do not cease to exist because they are ignored.' However, if a collection of completely reliable facts does not add up to bring out the truth, it's not because the truth wasn't included in the equation, but it is because the overriding fact was always accompanied by a shadow; and the shadow became longer as the source of light falling upon it moved away, and the defence lawyer knew how to play with the light to create these shadows.

In the case of State vs Kamala Prasad aka Munna, the court deemed that the chain of circumstantial evidence was too tenuous to stand up to conjecture, and so the defendant walked even as the police officers and the prosecutors were left licking their wounds.

A look at the crime statistics in India indicates a dismal picture when it comes to the success rate of achieving a conviction

[52] Harendra Singh Pal vs Sandeep Kumar and Ors on 14 July 2017 (indiankanoon.org).

of suspects who are tried. The success rate is just 57 per cent. Britain has a far more impressive record with 80 per cent. In Japan, it is over 99 per cent, and in China, under what is called the zero-acquittal policy, the conviction rate is 99.9 per cent. Russia too, has a conviction rate of 99 per cent. The philosophy of not convicting an accused if there is even the slightest of a reasonable doubt in the story presented by the prosecution guides jurisprudence in India and other democratic countries like the UK and the USA. Lawyers representing the accused persons often find that the existence of such doubts leads to acquittals.

Among other things, this data points to the need for direct evidence. The prosecutors' self-confidence takes a serious beating if merely circumstantial evidence is to be relied upon. It is well-known that many police officers are not averse to using torture during the interrogation of suspects, a method which is colloquially referred to as the third-degree, to extract certain statements that will lead to the strengthening of the prosecution's case. This has led to there being a provision in the Indian Evidence Act which says that anything stated before a police officer during an investigation does not qualify to be presented as evidence in a court of law.

The exception to this provision comes in the shape of Section 27 of the Indian Evidence Act. This section allows certain revelations made to a police officer during an investigation to qualify as admissible evidence.[53] This exception is very frequently

---

[53] Section 27 of the Indian Evidence Act: How much of information received from accused may be proved:

the go-to provision used by the police for the discovery of the murder weapon. It is often the case that the investigating officer is concerned deeply about finding the gun, dagger, or any other object that was used to cause the victim's death. The courts also lay emphasis on this piece of evidence. The accused is the person who is most likely to be aware of the location of the murder weapon. It is for this reason that the statement that leads to the discovery of the murder weapon is considered as admissible evidence in a court of law in India. The recovery of the plastic jar in Uthra's case was the key inflection point in the investigation. That the information was extracted from Sooraj without the use of any third-degree speaks highly of the merit and skill of the interrogators.

Otherwise, imagine a situation where the murder weapon is a living, breathing, and slithering one which can make up its own mind and keep changing its locations. The investigators in the Uthra murder case had to deal with this slippery reality. The evidence was, even otherwise, only circumstantial. That the case ended in conviction in the trial court brings to the fore the exceptional attention which was paid to all aspects of the investigation.

Provided that, when any fact is deposed to as discovered in consequence of information received from a person accused of any offence, in the custody of a police officer, so much of such information, whether it amounts to a confession or not, as relates distinctly to the fact thereby discovered, may be proved.

To look at something as saddening as the death of a human being and think of it as a transaction is certainly heartless. However, in legal parlance, even a murder could be classified as a transaction.

The Uthra murder case had two clear episodes that were separated by time and space. The first attempt on her life, which had fortunately failed, was made on the night of 2 March 2020. The second snakebite which Uthra succumbed to was inflicted on the night of 6 May 2020. The location of the first episode was Sooraj's house, Sree Surya, in Parakkodu, district Pathanamthitta. The fatal act happened in Uthra's parents' house, called Vishu House, located in Eram at Anchal in Kollam district.

The defence argued that the two episodes should have been treated as two distinct offences, committed on two different dates, at two different places, located in two separate districts; therefore, it was mandatory for two individual FIRs to have been registered for both the offences.

The prosecution, on the other hand, was clear that there was unity of purpose and design, as well as continuity in the actions of the accused. On both occasions, the intent was the same—to kill Uthra. The first attempt, made using a Russell's viper, had been deadly and Uthra barely survived it before she succumbed to the next attempt at envenomation using an Indian cobra.

The Supreme Court had laid down the law in this regard in the V. Cheemalapati Venkata Rao case.[54] The relevant extract

---

[54] State of Andhra Pradesh vs. Cheemalapati Venkata Rao, AIR 1963 SC 1850.

from this verdict is, '...it is generally thought that where there is proximity of time or place or unity of purpose and design or continuity of action in respect of a series of acts, it may be possible to infer that they form part of the same transaction. It is, however, not necessary that every one of these elements should coexist for a transaction to be regarded as the same. But if several acts committed by a person show a unity of purpose or design that would be a strong circumstance to indicate that those acts form part of the same transaction.'

Based on the above citation of the apex court, the trial court came to the conclusion that the two attempts that Sooraj made to kill Uthra were fit to be treated as the same transaction for which the registration of only one FIR was not an 'irregularity, illegality or material defect, which caused prejudice to the accused.'

In a recent case in Uttarakhand, Ankita Bhandari, a teenager who was serving as a receptionist at a resort near Rishikesh, was murdered on 18 September 2022, allegedly by her employer and his friends, in the Chila forest where her corpse was found in a canal six days after the fatal incident. The deceased was said to have repeatedly refused to accede to the demand for providing 'special services' (a euphemism for sexual services) to a VIP guest at the resort. This led to heated exchanges at the resort between the accused and the victim. The accused then asked Ankita to accompany them to another place to resolve the issue. It is said that there was no consensus that was reached, and the young receptionist had to pay the price with her life.

In this much discussed case, the incidents which commenced at the resort and culminated in the unfortunate end of a youngster's life at another spot, have all been seen as a single transaction and have been charge-sheeted after a thorough investigation by a Special Investigation Team.

Lokanath Behera, the director-general of police, Hari Sankar, the superintendent of police, Ashokan, the investigating officer, and other members of the SIT, all deserve great praise for their exemplary work. An investigation is built around the kernel of direct evidence and circumstantial evidence works as the glue that makes the prosecution's presentation incontestable. The Uthra murder case is already the subject matter of forensic science textbooks since the entire case was built around facts gleaned from the varying disciplines of science. It was a case which had no direct evidence, and yet the investigating team succeeded in putting together a water-tight presentation. No wonder the investigation drew widespread praise. A report in the e-paper *OnManorama* has observed, 'The incident, which shook Kerala, has now become part of the criminology syllabus. "Homicidal Snakebite" explains a natural weapon like a snake employed to commit a murder, and how to investigate such an incident. Each stage in the probe in the Uthra murder case has become a chapter in criminology.'[55]

---

55 'How smart investigation nailed Sooraj convincingly in Uthra case,' *OnManorama*.

For their exemplary work, the entire Crime Branch team received several accolades, including commendations from the director-general of police and badges of honour from the Kerala government. Hari Sankar and Ashokan were awarded the 'Union Home Minister's Medal for Excellence in Investigation' for the year 2021.[56]

[56] This medal was constituted in 2018, with the objective to promote high professional standards in the investigation of crimes and to recognise such excellence in investigation by investigating officers.

DOWRY DEATHS

A major element involved in Uthra's untimely demise was the exchange of dowry. Every undue financial instalment added fuel to the criminal fire that was raging within Sooraj. This book is an opportunity to briefly understand this critical problem.

Nineteen women succumb to dowry related crimes in India every day. The Dowry Prohibition Act (1961) is now six decades old. However, the archaic tradition continues to plague large tracts of not just rural but also educated urban India.

Data from the National Crime Records Bureau (NCRB) tabled by the Union Minister of State for Home, Ajay Kumar Mishra, in December 2022 in the Rajya Sabha revealed some startling numbers: 35,493 dowry deaths were reported in India between 2017 and 2021. In 2017, as many as 7,466 dowry deaths were reported. This number was 7,167 in 2018, 7,141 in 2019, 6,966 in 2020, and 6,753 in 2021.[57] These numbers are not just alarming, but they must be understood in the context of being heavily undercounted as well. It is no secret

[57] '35,493 Dowry Deaths Reported Between 2017–21; 20 Deaths Daily: Govt Data,' *Outlook India.*

that many cases of dowry deaths are brushed under the carpet by the victim's family to save face and maintain their supposed social dignity.

According to the Dowry Prohibition Act, 'dowry means any property or valuable security given or agreed to be given either directly or indirectly:

a. by one party to a marriage to the other party to the marriage; or
b. by the parents of either party to a marriage or by any other person, to either party to the marriage or to any other person; at or before or any time after the marriage in connection with the marriage of said parties but does not include *dower* or *mahr* in the case of persons to whom the Muslim Personal Law (*Shariat*) applies.[58]

The police have the power to make arrests in cases where domestic violence is reported, under Section 498A of the IPC. Under Section 304B of the IPC, those found guilty of causing a dowry death may face a prison term of seven years to life imprisonment.

The sentence that even a mere demand for dowry carries is extendable up to several years in prison. In spite of the large duration and the magnitude of potential punishments prescribed in the law, the age-old custom of dowry is still rampant in India. In fact, even the families of law enforcers themselves have been found guilty of the offence.

A World Bank study showed, on the basis of a sample, that dowry was exchanged in 95 per cent of the 40,000 (sample

---

[58] The Dowry Prohibition Act, 1961 (indiankanoon.org).

size) marriages that took place in rural India between 1960 and 2008. The information was based on the 2006 Rural Economic and Demographic Survey, the most recent source of dowry data covering seventeen major states of the country.[59]

Low conviction rates in courts of law are a part of the problem. Conviction rates of cases under Section 498A of the IPC slipped from 21.9 per cent in 2006 to 13 per cent in 2018. From 2018 to 2020, thirty-four cases of dowry deaths were registered in the state of Kerala alone. None had seen a conviction till August 2021. Clearly, justice is often delayed and therefore, denied. Out-of-court settlements are reached and cases are often dropped when they stretch across several years.

The Ministry of Women and Child Development undertakes awareness exercises for the safety and security of women. Further, the central government, through institutions like the National Commission for Women, has been organising seminars and on-the-ground workshops to sensitise people across the gender spectrum about the evils of the dowry system and also about the various provisions of law that forbid this age-old custom.

Stricter laws and rising awareness have, however, not translated into tangible results. Dowry is a nightmare that the women of our country live with through the course of their lives. The solution lies at the tenuous junction of the logic inherent in law and the emotional intelligence carried by society. There

59 'India dowry disputes: Families in Kerala are at war over a wedding tradition banned decades ago,' CNN.

have been instances when the two have come together to deliver a revolution. It will take another revolution to eradicate the menace of dowry deaths. Only then will the Uthras of the world stand a better chance.

As the ideas of romance, love, and companionship assume more inclusive dimensions, our laws must evolve accordingly. The rewording of Acts like those which prohibit dowry is inevitable in the long run, but the groundwork for this rework should have begun yesterday!

BEYOND THE MYTHS

Kerala is often called God's Own Country. The natural beauty of the state has earned it this moniker. The forests are lush, the rivers always gush, and the sounds of its animals never hush.

The rhyme in the previous sentence may be an unsuccessful attempt at both poetry and describing Kerala, but its meaning can be taken quite literally. Kerala is a certified hotspot of biodiversity. It has an enviable abundance of natural wealth. And where there is nature, there are always its most adept and evolved creations. Snakes are no exception to this rule.

An exhaustive chapter on snakes would not serve the larger purpose of penning this book. However, an overview of the types of venomous snakes found in Kerala is essential for understanding the human-animal interface. While almost all venomous species of snakes found in India are also found in Kerala, there are five which are more commonly found in the state and which also pose a credible threat to the human population. These include the Indian cobra, the king cobra, the Russell's viper, the saw-scaled viper, and the krait.

Indian Cobra

Scientific Name: *Naja naja*

Malayalam Name: *Moorkhan*

One of the most fabled creatures from mythological times, the Indian cobra truly lives up to its sinister reputation. The signature hood which the snake forms by raising the skin on either side of its neck is for many synonymous with the very idea of fear. The hood on its dorsal side bears a characteristic mark which has found its way into traditional works of art across the country. Saree prints commonly feature this design which looks like a spectacle.

The snake is highly poisonous and can grow up to six feet in length. It is usually found in open forests and farmlands. It also frequents abandoned rat holes and termite mounds. Cobras are natural swimmers and can take to water very effortlessly. They feed on small prey like rodents, lizards, and frogs.

The venom of the cobra is neurotoxic and directly impacts the central nervous system. The Oriental Rat snake, *Ptyas mucosus*, is often mistaken for the cobra; however, this snake is much longer and can easily be told apart from the Indian cobra by the stronger ridged appearance of its body. Other snakes which resemble the *Naja naja* are the Banded Racer or the *Argyrogena fasciolata* and the Indian Smooth Snake or the *Coronella brachyura*.

King Cobra

Scientific Name: *Naja hannah*

Malayalam Name: *Rajavembala*

To say that the king cobra is the undisputed king of the Indian snake kingdom is not an overstatement. Everything about the snake is princely, including the kind of territory it commands.

The king cobra is usually found in thick forests and can measure up to fifteen feet in length. Unlike the Indian cobra, the hood of the king cobra has no distinctive markings. Its venom is neurotoxic and is injected by the snake using its half-inch fangs. The toxic compounds present in the venom impact the central nervous system, and in many cases cause irreparable damage and even lead to the death of the individual.

King cobras are the only snakes in the world that build nests for their eggs. They zealously guard their nests until the hatchlings emerge.

The diet of the king cobra consists primarily of other cold-blooded animals, particularly other snakes. Some cobras develop a diet specific to one species of snake. Among the various species that the king cobra feeds on, the rat snake is the most preferred. In rare circumstances of food scarcity, king cobras hunt vertebrates and lizards.

Russell's Viper

Scientific Name: *Vipera russelli*

Malayalam Name: *Mandali, Rakthamandali, Manchatti*

In terms of danger levels, the Russell's viper is India's deadliest snake. It does not enjoy the criminal reputation of the cobra, but it accounts for a far greater number of human lives.[60] Dorsally, the colour pattern on the snake consists of a deep yellow, tan, or brown, with three series of dark brown spots that run the length of its body. The snake is a persistent hisser. It typically has a length that ranges from four to five feet. This snake is viviparous (gives birth to live offspring).

The habitat of the Russell's viper is diverse, but the snake tends to avoid dense forests and humid environments like marshes. It is a highly urbanised species and is often found near human settlements where rodents are available in plenty.

The venom of the Russell's viper is hemotoxic, as in it affects the blood vascular system, destroys blood cells and blood vessels, and causes internal bleeding. It is a nocturnal hunter and preys primarily on rodents. It waits for its prey to get close before injecting a lethal dose of venom. It swallows the prey whole once it's dead. This snake frequently ventures down burrows in search of food and may enter homes when seeking out rats.

Saw-Scaled Viper

Scientific Name: *Echis carinatus*

Malayalam Name: *Anali*

The name *Echis* is the Latin transliteration of the Greek word for viper. This snake grows up to a length of two to three feet. The saw-scaled viper has a pale buff, greyish, reddish, olive, or pale brown ground colour. It has an overlaid mid-dorsal with a series

---

[60] 'Poisonous snakes,' kerenvis.nic.in

of variably coloured but mostly whitish spots that are edged with dark brown and separated by lighter inter-blotch patches.[61] The head of the saw-scaled viper is triangular and distinct from the neck. It bears a white arrow mark. The snake has a unique threat display—rubbing sections of its body together to produce a sizzling sound.

The venom of the snake is hemotoxic and has great medicinal value. It is used in the manufacture of several drugs, including some widely used anticoagulants. Saw-scaled vipers are highly aggressive compared to many of their cousins and they commonly strike to bite.

The diet of the saw-scaled vipers in extremely varied and includes locusts, beetles, worms, slugs, spiders, scorpions, centipedes, solifugids, frogs, toads, reptiles (including other snakes), small mammals, and birds.

Krait

Scientific Name: *Bungarus caeruleus*

Malayalam Name: *Vellikettan, Mothiravalayan, Ettadi Veeran, Ettadi Moorkhan, Samkhuvarayan*

The krait is a highly venomous snake with many species. The most common species found in Kerala is the *Bungarus Caeruleus* which is blue or dark bluish grey in colour with white crossbars. It lives in a wide variety of habitats, from fields and low scrub

---

[61] 'Indian Saw-Scaled Viper – Facts, Diet, Habitat & Pictures,' Animalia.bio

jungles to settled areas. It rests in termite mounds, brick piles, rat holes, and even inside houses.[62]

Krait venom is neurotoxic. The snake's diet comprises small mammals, frogs, and lizards. When agitated, it coils up with its head concealed and body flattened, and makes jerky movements. It may also lift its tail. It is reluctant to bite, but when it does, it typically holds on for a while, which enables it to inject considerable amounts of venom into the body of its victim. It is notorious for its appetite for other snakes and frequently consumes blind snakes and other species, including other members of the genus *bungarus*. When in pursuit of rodents, it often ends up inside human dwellings.[63]

The four venomous snake species which are responsible for causing the greatest number of potentially fatal human snakebites in the Indian subcontinent (majorly in India) are the Russell's viper, the common krait, the Indian cobra, and the saw-scaled viper. These snakes are collectively referred to as the Big Four.

According to the Ministry of Health and Family Welfare, there is a huge gap between the number of snakebite deaths reported in direct surveys and the official data. A meagre 7 per cent of snakebite deaths are officially reported. Annual snakebite deaths are greatest in the states of Uttar Pradesh, Andhra Pradesh, and

---

62 http://www.toxinology.com/fusebox.cfm?fuseaction=main.snakes.display&id=SN0015

63 Poisonous snakes (kerenvis.nic.in).

Bihar. Other Indian states with a high number of similar cases are Tamil Nadu, West Bengal, Maharashtra, and Kerala.

General awareness about snakebites is essential to reducing mortality. In 2004, the WHO provided recommendations to reduce deaths due to envenomation. A primary recommendation that relies on evidence-based procedures, was to establish a single protocol for both first-aid and treatment, and is relevant in the Indian context as well.

The first-aid protocol that is currently recommended by the WHO may be remembered by the mnemonic **CARRY NO R.I.G.H.T.**[64]

CARRY: Do not let the victim walk even for a short distance. The victim must be transported in a vehicle or be carried, especially when the bite is on the legs.

NO:

No tourniquet.

No cutting.

No electrotherapy.

No pressure immobilisation or nitric oxide donor (Nitroglycerin ointment/nitrate spray).

R.I.G.H.T:

R: Reassure the patient. Reassurance will drive away their fear and excitement, slow the patient's heart rate, and reduce the spread of venom. About 70 per cent of all snakebites are by non-venomous species and of the bites by venomous snakes, only 50 per cent actually poison the victims.

---

64 'First Aid,' National Health Portal of India (nhp.gov.in).

I: Immobilise the patient's entire body by laying him/her down in a comfortable and safe position, ideally in the recovery position (lying prone on the left side in case vomiting threatens to lead to aspiration), and immobilise the bitten limb with a splint or a sling. Any movement or muscular contraction, caused, for example, by undressing the victim or making them walk, will increase the absorption and spread of venom by squeezing the veins and the lymphatics. Do not apply pressure and ensure that blood supply is unhindered. Compression in the form of tight ligatures does not work and may prove, instead, to be dangerous.

GH (Government Hospital): The patient must be transported to a place where they can receive medical care (dispensary or hospital) as quickly, but as safely and comfortably as possible. If possible, patients should be placed in the recovery position during transit, in case they vomit.

T: Try and extract a precise history of the circumstances of the bite and the progression of symptoms while on the way to the hospital.

Four useful initial questions are:

1. 'What part of your body were you bitten in? Point to the place.'

   Observe any local signs around the wound site such as fang marks, swelling, bruising, persistent bleeding, pre-hospital traditional treatment.

2. 'When were you bitten and what were you doing when you were bitten?'

   If the patient was bitten at night while asleep, then in all probability, it was a krait; if the patient was bitten in a paddy field, it was likely to have been a cobra or a Russell's viper; if while tending fruit trees, a green pit viper; if while swimming or wading in water, a cobra (fresh water) or sea snake (sea or estuary).

3. 'Where is the snake that bit you?' or 'What did it look like? Did anyone take a picture?'

   If the snake has been killed and brought along, or if an adequately clear photograph is available (e.g. taken by a mobile phone camera at the scene of the bite), its correct identification can be very helpful. If it is an obviously harmless species (or not a snake at all!), the patient can be quickly reassured and discharged from the hospital. If it was killed and left at home, send someone to fetch it, in whatever condition it might be!

4. 'How are you feeling now? Have any symptoms of envenoming developed?'

   A common early symptom of systemic envenoming is vomiting and, in the case of being bitten by some specific species, fainting and collapsing (sometimes causing injury) with transient unconsciousness and features of anaphylaxis. Patients who become defibrinogenated or thrombocytopenic may begin to bleed from old, partially healed wounds while also bleeding persistently from the fang marks. The patient should be asked how much urine they have passed since the bite and whether it was a normal colour or very dark (implying haemoglobin/myoglobinurea). Patients who complain of sleepiness, drooping eyelids or blurred or double vision may have neurotoxic envenoming. An important early symptom of sea snake envenoming that may develop as soon as 30 minutes after the bite is generalised pain, tenderness and stiffness of muscles, and trismus.

Note: Do not waste time in first-aid management by traditional methods which may dangerously delay effective treatment. Constricting bands or tourniquets may cause pain, swelling, and congestion that suggest local envenoming. Ingested herbal remedies may cause vomiting. Instillation of irritant plant juices into the eyes may cause conjunctivitis. Forcible insufflation of oils into the respiratory tract may lead to aspiration pneumonia, bronchospasm, ruptured ear drums, and pneumothorax. Incisions, cauterisation, immersion in scalding liquid, and heating over a fire can result in devastating injuries.

Unfortunately, only a small fraction of bite victims seek help from a trained doctor in a hospital or a dispensary. A slightly larger number seek assistance from village doctors, while most still use the services of traditional *ojhas*.[65]

Victims of snakebites are not just commonly misdiagnosed as suffering from a variety of ailments such as indigestion, appendicitis, stroke, head injury, ischemic heart disease, food poisoning, trismus, hysteria, and Guillain-Barré syndrome, but they are also subjected to unnecessary investigations including

[65] Guidance for the management of snakebites, WHO (2016).

MRI scans, all of which lead to unwanted delays in the administration of anti-venom.[66]

Compounding the problem are the century-old manufacturing protocols for anti-venom in India. A polyvalent anti-venom is produced for protection against the Big Four snakes—the Indian cobra, the common krait, the Russell's viper, and the saw-scaled viper. However, in addition to these snakes, India is home to many other species of venomous snakes that have the potential to inflict deadly, even fatal bites. About sixty of the 270 species of Indian snakes are considered medically important. But specific anti-venoms are not produced against these species; instead, the Big Four anti-venom is routinely used to treat all snakebites.

A recent paper by a team of scientists from the Indian Institute of Science found polyvalent anti-venom to be grossly inefficient in overcoming the effects of toxins in the venom of neglected snake species. The study underlined a pressing need for manufacturers, public health officials, and policymakers to wake up to the need of developing region-specific snakebite therapies.[67]

Pop culture has done great injustice to the image of snakes in India. The general sense that one gets from mainstream cinema

---

[66] Management of Snakebite, Ministry of Health & Family Welfare (2016).

[67] 'Snake venom study reveals troubling shortcomings in anti-venom therapy in India', Indian Institute of Science.

is of the *Nagin* kind. Every serpent is either looked at with suspicion or superstition. Sooraj tried to capitalise on the sarpa dosha belief and even succeeded for a while.

The use of snakes as murder weapons takes us farther away from recognising our role in these crimes. The understanding that one builds about snakes through our educational curriculums is minimal. Snakes are seen as being dangerous and are almost always killed if they venture into people's homes. The need of the hour is to educate people about how the interface between man and snake is an integral part of our survival. The education must not be limited to presentations alone, but must be expanded to include actual contact with the species. This beautiful scaled creature must get its due for we have done way too much harm in its name. The forked human tongue needs to live up to the promised efforts of conservation and awareness!

EPILOGUE

Ronald Reagan had said, 'For too long, the victims of crime have been the forgotten persons of our criminal justice system.'

Crime is no cops-and-robbers game. It has dimensions which go way beyond those that appear apparent at first sight; or even the subsequent ones.

Even sensational cases which grab the headlines, die down and fall out of public memory. The fact is, we do not go beyond the obvious.

In Uthra's tragic end, we can conclude with a degree of justification that we know who the victims are. Of course, all the lists will commence with Uthra's name, the one who lost her life after a long period of maltreatment at the hands of the man who had taken vows to protect her for life and be her companion in all victories and travails.

The names of Uthra's grieving parents, Manimekhala and Vijayasenan will come next, and her brother Vishu will be right there at the top too.

But quite possibly, many will forget little Dhruv, who was just an infant when the tragedy struck. As the years pass, he will miss the love that only a mother can give to her child. He may never receive the protection and love of his other parent, Sooraj, either. Will he grow up as an individual who is emotionally at peace? It seems highly unlikely. What does seem probable is that he will be bitter about the misfortune that the cruel ways of the world brought into his life. Will he learn about the all-important human values of kindness and love? Will he respect the society of which he is a member? Will Dhruv shine like the star he is named after? Or will he be a rebel? Only time will tell.

Victims rarely, if ever, get true justice. And this needs to change. But how and in what form this change will come about, and who will be the harbinger of this change are things that are unpredictable. It seems too remote a possibility to happen in the tangible future.

These thoughts are troubling. But there is some solace to be found in the fact that Dhruv's mother was one of those fortunate few whom the screeching wheels of the Indian criminal justice system did not run over! On the contrary, she was triumphantly carried over the line.

THE KEY PLAYERS

	**Hari Sankar** 2020: Superintendent of Police, Kollam Rural Now: Assistant Inspector-General, Police Headquarters
	**S. Madhusoodanan** 2020: Additional SP, Kollam Rural Now: Superintendent of Police, Crime Branch
	**A. Ashokan** 2020: Deputy SP, District Crime Branch, Kollam Rural Now: Retired
	**Anoop Krishna R. P.** 2020: Inspector of Police Now: Inspector of Police
	**Advocate Mohan Raj** Special Prosecutor

ACKNOWLEDGEMENTS

This sensational case had been widely covered in the media, especially the Malayalam electronic and print media. It has since been tried at the District Court, and the perpetrator has been handed out due punishment.

What the two of us felt was an absence of the true appreciation of a historic effort on the part of the Kerala police in the investigation of this diabolical murder and the great contribution made by the team of experts and forensic scientists in pinning the culprit. It is for this reason that *Fangs of Death* has been written.

Our literary agent Suhail Mathur of The Book Bakers has been instrumental in finding our wonderful publisher, Amaryllis. The editor, Bidisha Srivastava, has made significant contributions to our manuscript. We are grateful to them both.

We must acknowledge the ready help we have received from officers of Kerala police, especially AIG Hari Sankar IPS and Additional SP (retired) A. Ashokan who provided details we required, including the photographs we have used in the book. We are also thankful to DGP (retired) Lokanath Behera for the help he has rendered.

ABOUT THE AUTHORS

Maanas Lal has built a formidable reputation across genres of art. Apart from penning hundreds of columns for the print media, he is the co-author of *Murder in the Bylanes: Life and Death in a Divided City* and *On the Trail of Thugs and Thieves: True Accounts of Crime from the Hindi Heartland.* His work in the fields of painting, photography and digital art has found collectors across the globe. A software engineer, he has used his expertise in technology to develop a unique style of digital painting. He holds soft skills workshops in India's leading schools and professional institutions. He is a TEDx speaker. He is also the secretary of the Doon Cultural and Literary Society.

A gold medallist IIT-ian, **Aloke Lal** joined the IPS in 1975. He served for thirty-seven years in the khaki, rising to the top rank of director-general. He received two medals from the President of India—one for 'long and meritorious services' and the other for 'distinguished services'. He is the author of *The Barabanki Narcos: Busting India's Most Notorious Drug Cartel* and co-author of *Murder in the Bylanes: Life and Death in a Divided City* and *On the Trail of Thugs and Thieves: True Accounts of Crime from the Hindi Heartland.* A TEDx speaker, Aloke is festival director of the Crime Literature Festival of India.